www.wadsworth.com

wadsworth.com is the World Wide Web site for Wadsworth and is your direct source to dozens of online resources.

At *wadsworth.com* you can find out about supplements, demonstration software, and student resources. You can also send email to many of our authors and preview new publications and exciting new technologies.

wadsworth.com
Changing the way the world learns®

A Practical Handbook for
WRITING IN THE HUMANITIES

••••••••••••••••

MICHAEL C. MILAM

University of South Florida

••••••••••••••••

THOMSON
— ✳ —
™
WADSWORTH

Australia • Canada • Mexico • Singapore • Spain
United Kingdom • United States

THOMSON

WADSWORTH

Publisher: Clark Baxter
Acquisitions Editor: John Swanson
Assistant Editor: Amy McGaughey
Editorial Assistant: Rebecca Jackson
Technology Project Manager:
  Melinda Newfarmer
Marketing Manager: Mark Orr
Advertising Project Manager: Vicky Chao
Production Project Manager: Matt Ballantyne
Print/Media Buyer: Doreen Suruki
Permissions Editor: Charles Hodgkins

Production Service: Forbes Mill Press
Text Designer: Robin Gold
Photo Researcher: Amy McGaughey
Copy Editor: Robin Gold
Cover Designer: Carole Lawson
Cover Image: Jacques-Louis David, *Oath of the Horatii*, 1784. Used by permission of Reunion des Musees Nationaux, Paris/Art Resource, New York.
Compositor: Forbes Mill Press
Text and Cover Printer: Webcom Limited

Printed in Canada
2 3 4 5 6 7 06 05 04

For more information about our products, contact us at:
Thomson Learning Academic Resource Center
1-800-423-0563
For permission to use material from this text, contact us by:
Phone: 1-800-730-2214
Fax: 1-800-730-2215
Web: http://www.thomsonrights.com

Library of Congress Control Number:
2002107736

ISBN 0-15-505015-X

Wadsworth/Thomson Learning
10 Davis Drive
Belmont, CA 94002-3098
USA

Asia
Thomson Learning
5 Shenton Way #01-01
UIC Building
Singapore 068808

Australia
Nelson Thomson Learning
102 Dodds Street
South Melbourne, Victoria 3205
Australia

Canada
Nelson Thomson Learning
1120 Birchmount Road
Toronto, Ontario M1K 5G4
Canada

Europe/Middle East/Africa
Thomson Learning
High Holborn House
50/51 Bedford Row
London WC1R 4LR
United Kingdom

Latin America
Thomson Learning
Seneca, 53
Colonia Polanco
11560 Mexico D.F.
Mexico

Spain
Paraninfo Thomson Learning
Calle/Magallanes, 25
28015 Madrid, Spain

Contents

·················
Preface
·················

A Practical Handbook for Writing in the Humanities is the result of a number of years of grading essays by undergraduate college students who possess rudimentary writing skills. In fact, most new students at colleges and universities are not well prepared to write on a college level. To address this problem in my humanities classes, I created and developed a series of handouts concerning format, style, and other matters relevant to college writing. The handouts addressed only those skills that the students needed to write correctly. This was based on a knowledge gained from the direct experience of grading papers, an understanding free of composition theory. Therefore, the purpose of the handouts was entirely practical; they were designed to teach students to organize an essay, write clear and concise sentences, and use a proper format, and to do so with the least amount of time and effort possible while still writing a college-level paper that is grammatically and rhetorically correct. In other words, I reduced the necessary rules and skills to the fewest possible number so that the students could concentrate on the essentials. Eventually, the handouts turned into a practical handbook that many of my students have used throughout their college years with great success. Thus, my students proved to me the assumption behind this handbook: most students are motivated, and if they are given clear objectives and presented with the required steps, they can improve their writing to the college level in a relatively short period of time. I thank each and every one of my students from Indiana University, Tampa College, St. Petersburg College, The State University of Irkutsk, Russia, and the University of South Florida. I certainly have learned as much from them as they have from me.

Others whom I should like to thank are the instructors who, with their own classroom experience in mind, reviewed this text and helped me shape what it is. They are Kimberly Felos, St. Petersburg College; Scott Douglass, Chattanooga State Technical College; Bruce Hozeski, Ball State University; Joe Law, Wright State University; Karen Styles, Valencia Community College; and Michael Walensky, Diablo Valley College. I would also like to thank Janice Walker of Georgia Southern University.

Finally, thanks to my editorial team at Wadsworth Publishing: John Swanson, Acquisitions Editor; Amy McGaughey, Assistant Editor; Matt Ballantyne, Production Project Manager; and Robin Gold of Forbes Mill Press, copyeditor and production.

As always, I dedicate the work to Pam, Jennifer, Amanda, and Julie.

Introduction

The major assumption behind *A Practical Handbook for Writing in the Humanities* is that in structure and style the simple undocumented essay and the research paper have virtually no differences beyond the research and documentation of sources. Both should rely on the paragraph-by-paragraph development of a thesis, and both should rely on an objective, depersonalized tone that emphasizes the correct use of standard American English and consistent logic. To that purpose, this handbook is designed as a textbook and as a student handbook to teach the basic structure and style of college writing—the formal essay. The handbook may be employed by writing instructors as a simple and basic method to teach composition, or students may use it without an instructor's help. (The handbook is especially meant for the students of humanities instructors who require writing assignments but have no time to give formal instruction in composition.) To achieve this dual purpose, the book aims at brevity. Most composition handbooks are large because they include all rules and possible cases. Although such handbooks are necessary, they are often intimidating to new students, or they are difficult for students to use without instruction. This handbook is designed to offer the student only the essentials presented in a simple and direct manner.

As a teaching approach, the formal essay offers a structure that encourages the student to concentrate on unity and coherence in paragraphs controlled by the thesis and topic sentences. Hence, the focus is on the student's ability to organize ideas into well-developed paragraphs. To facilitate writing and rewriting, the handbook provides all the basic tools including sample theses, sample analyses of poetry and painting, format examples, a sample outline, sample papers, suggestions on style, suggestions for writing clear and concise sentences, and a section on the punctuation of titles and dates appropriate for all disciplines in the humanities. Finally, short and basic sections are given on library research, online research, and the use and documentation of sources with sample footnotes/endnotes and bibliographic entries in both the MLA and Chicago styles and the Columbia style for online documentation. The formal essay has been separated from the research paper so that students only concerned with formal essays will not have to confront the vagaries of documentation.

As a handbook, *A Practical Handbook for Writing in the Humanities* is designed to be used by the student without any instruction. Thus, the rules and examples are kept to a minimum so that, on the one hand, the student is not overwhelmed and, on the other hand, the student can quickly and easily find information needed while writing. The suggestions for structure, format, and punctuation should be acceptable for most college writing assignments, and the various sections are brief and, I hope, to the point. An index is included for quick reference that should be handy for the student during the writing process.

....

Instructions for the Student

....

This handbook is designed to help you write a formal essay in correct academic style in conjunction with or without classroom instruction. You should follow the approach outlined here to get the most out of this handbook.

1. "The Formal Essay" introduces the basic structure. Therefore, you should read and study this section first.

2. "Preparing to Write: Critical Thinking" begins the process of composing a formal essay.

3. "The First Step: The Thesis" helps you to decide what you will write about your topic. Examples of theses are given and analyzed so that you have a way to evaluate your own thesis.

4. The "Sample Analysis: Poetry" and "Sample Analysis: Painting" sections demonstrate the manner in which you may analyze poetry and paintings in preparation for developing your thesis and outline.

5. "Preparing the Structure: The Outline" explains how you may organize your ideas into paragraphs in a formal essay. At this point, you should go back and reread "The Formal Essay" in preparation for writing your paper. Before you write your paper, you will also want to read the "Sample Paper in MLA Style" and the "Sample Research Paper in MLA Style" (ignoring the documentation matter for now) to get an idea of how your paper should be structured. While you are writing your paper, you will want to refer to "Notes on Format and Style" and "Punctuation of Titles, Names, and Other Matters," which cover many questions students have concerning punctuation and style. While writing, however, you should not be too concerned with the format itself.

6. The "Editing and Rewriting" and "Sentence Punctuation" sections give instructions on how to restructure paragraphs and to write clear and concise sentences. You will want to consult them during the writing process.

7. "Preparing the Final Product: The Format" should be consulted after you have written your paper. This section will explain to you the proper manner in which to prepare the paper before you submit the final product to your instructor.

8. "Editing and Rewriting," "Sentence Punctuation," and "Grading Abbreviations, Words, and Symbols" should help you to evaluate and correct your work if your instructor asks you to rewrite your paper.

9. The "soul" of this handbook is the instruction on writing a formal essay. However, the handbook is also designed to guide you through the research, writing, and documentation of a research paper. When you need to write a research paper, you should study the process of the formal essay first; then the research paper sections can be read in succession and should be self-explanatory.

10. Finally, there are appendixes on studying, reading literature, reading textbooks, taking notes, and answering an essay question. My students always appreciate these little tips, so I would like to pass them on to you.

Part One
Essay Structure

· · · · · · · · · · · · · · · ·

Section 1
The Formal Essay
· · · · · · · · · · · · · · · ·

The **formal essay** is argumentative. That is, it takes a position on a subject and argues that position against other positions on the subject. The formal essay is persuasive. It attempts to persuade the reader to accept the writer's position using standard American English and the consistent use of logic.

Structure

Although experienced writers may structure arguments in a variety of ways, the following is suggested as a convenient, ready-made thesis approach for inexperienced writers.

1. *Introduction:* The introduction should give the reader any information necessary for understanding the thesis or placing the thesis in context. The introduction might define key terms or limit the scope of the paper, for example.

2. *Thesis:* The **thesis** should clearly state the *limited topic,* the *writer's position* toward the topic, and the *direction* the paper will take—that is, in what manner the thesis will be defended. This should be done, ideally, in one sentence. In short essays, the introduction and thesis constitute the first paragraph with the latter being the final sentence. The thesis is the most crucial part of the formal essay because a clear thesis promotes a clear argument—a comprehensible paper that adheres closely to the topic and writer's position.

3. *Support Paragraphs:* Each paragraph should develop *one major point of the argument.* Each paragraph will contain a *topic sentence,* which is the idea of the paragraph. This idea should relate directly to, or support, the thesis and be developed and explained by the other sentences of that paragraph. A good support paragraph, then, should demonstrate *unity* and *coherence.* **Unity** exists when all sentences in the paragraph directly

discuss the topic sentence. When there is clear thought and logical connections between all sentences, the paragraph is said to possess **coherence** or good sentence connection.

4. *Transition Sentences*: A *transition sentence* should come at the end of each paragraph to connect the main idea of one paragraph to the next. Transition sentences hold together the logic of the argument because they connect the main ideas of each paragraph and demonstrate their connection to the thesis.

5. *Conclusion*: The conclusion should not summarize. The formal essay is usually not long; therefore, a summary often appears repetitious to the reader. Instead, the conclusion should point out the *significance* of the argument. That is, it should relate the thesis to a larger issue. The conclusion should become more important as the writer becomes more experienced; hence, it is less important for the inexperienced writer who should concentrate on the structure of the argument itself.

Style

1. The formal essay should have a disinterested, objective tone. Words should be used in their denotative (dictionary) meanings.

2. "I," "you," and "we" should be avoided. The third person ("he, "she," "it," and "they") is the proper form.

3. The strength of the argument must rest on fact, logic, and clear expression of ideas. It follows, then, that slang, humor, metaphor, and clichés should be avoided.

4. Questions, whether rhetorical or otherwise, should be avoided.

5. Exclamation points, exotic ink colors, nonstandard font styles, and any other text enhancements not required by standard practice should be avoided.

Writing and Reading

The formal essay as a pedagogical tool is designed to make students aware of structure in their writing and conscious of how the correct use of standard American English and the consistent use of logic create meaning and influence the reader. As a result, the lessons learned from the writing of formal essays should be readily applicable to other writing projects and to reading. If students become proficient in writing theses and structuring language into arguments, they should be able to recognize the major point, argument, and structure (if such exists) in what they read. Therefore, the student should become a better reader through understanding the basic structure of writing.

······················

Section 2
Preparing to Write: Critical Thinking
······················

College writing is not an intuitive skill or a mystical gift that some students naturally possess and others will just as naturally never possess. Often, a student will say, "I am not a good writer" or "She is just a natural writer, and I am not." This attitude is a misconception by the student because good writers are not born writers. Instead, writing is a skill acquired through the application of critical thinking, trial and error, and practice. *Any student who learns to think critically and to write clear, concise and grammatically correct sentences can write well in college.* The following is a description of critical thinking and its application to writing which is the process underlying the structure of the formal essay.

Critical thinking involves the ability to analyze a subject, distinguish between fact and opinion, recognize the importance of evidence, and consistently apply logic.

Analyzing a Subject

Analyzing a subject is to isolate and consider its various components, so you can understand the subject in a profound manner. In the humanities, this process is mainly concerned with the structure and meaning of works of art and literature in their cultural context.

A work of art—a novel, poem, painting, sculpture, play, musical composition—is usually analyzed by *form* and *content*, and these broad categories break down into smaller ones. *Formal elements* relate to the structure of a work, and *content* relates to the meaning of a work in the broadest sense.

The following are some elements in painting, poetry, and the novel (**note:** These are not exhaustive):

Painting:	Formal Elements:	Composition, Color, Lighting, Brushwork, Style
	Content:	Theme, Period, Cultural Context
Poetry:	Formal Elements:	Diction, Rhyme, Meter, Stanzaic Form, Style
	Content:	Theme, Period, Cultural Context
Novel:	Formal Elements:	Plot, Diction, Point of View, Style
	Content:	Theme, Period, Cultural Context

Another way to see this is to consider the *content*, or *meaning*, as the ideas expressed in the work—either the ideas expressed by the artist or author, or the ideas that the work expresses concerning its specific period

3

and culture. The *formal elements,* then, are the features that make the work of art precisely a novel, painting or sculpture, including the personal style of the artist or author (the unique manner in which that artist uses the formal elements). The formal elements *contain* the meaning.

An analysis, then, applies a set of criteria (standards of judgment and evaluation) to a work of art to understand the work's form and meaning. Novels have plots, paintings have compositions, and poems have stanzaic forms. All artists and authors have ideas that are expressed in their creations, and all art works are created in a specific time period and cultural context. Therefore, to think about how these elements work in individual paintings, sculptures, musical compositions, poems, and novels; to understand how the formal elements create meaning; and to compare these elements in different works is to do analysis in the humanities. (See Section 4, "Sample Analysis: Poetry," and Section 5, "Sample Analysis: Painting.")

Statements about the formal elements of a work are *usually* matters of fact or can be readily demonstrated whereas statements about the meaning of a work are opinions, requiring evidence to be convincing.

Formal Element: Dante's *Divine Comedy* is a first-person narrative.

Dante's epic is told in the first person by the character Dante, so this is a factual statement about a formal element of the work.

Content: Dante's *Divine Comedy* demonstrates the late medieval attitude toward Christian sin and redemption.

This is a statement about the content, the meaning, of the work in the cultural context of late medieval western Europe. Dante's epic certainly seems to be about sin and redemption. However, there is no *simple proof* that this specific work demonstrates the late medieval attitude toward Christian sin and redemption. This point could be (and has been) demonstrated, but the demonstration requires much evidence both from within the epic itself and from outside the epic by, for instance, works relating to the late medieval attitude toward sin and redemption. Because the demonstration is complex, and may be accomplished by different scholars from diverse perspectives and with the use of various evidence, the point is an opinion and will remain an opinion.

Distinguishing Between Fact and Opinion

As just described with Dante's *Divine Comedy,* a fact can be proven beyond reasonable doubt whereas an opinion can never be proven beyond doubt. An opinion is, therefore, made convincing through persuasive support.

So many of the subjects of Picasso's works were women because the artist was obsessed with his many relationships with women.

That Picasso created many artworks in which the subject was a woman is a fact that can be proven by simply looking over his works. However, that Picasso was obsessed with his relationships with women is an opinion inferred from this fact, not a fact in itself. There could very well be many other reasons to explain Picasso's use of women as subjects of his art. Nevertheless, this opinion could become a convincing opinion if it were supported by more evidence, for instance, relevant facts about his life, statements that he made about his art and women, and other biographical information.

Recognizing the Importance of Evidence

Evidence, often called "support" in writing, consists of the facts, testimony, examples, and other information that are used to support aspects of the thesis.

Testimony

> According to his notebooks, Dostoevsky based his character Shatov in *The Devils* on the Russian nihilist student I. Ivanov.

Whether or not Dostoevsky, *in fact,* based his character on I. Ivanov can never be proven. Fiction is not reality, and developing a character in a novel is a complex task. This is a point that could never be proven beyond doubt. Nevertheless, the fact that Dostoevsky suggests in his notebooks that I. Ivanov was the inspiration for Shatov is strong and convincing evidence in the form of *testimony* by the author.

Examples

> Linear perspective is a major element in Jacques-Louis David's Neoclassicism, and this technique for giving the illusion of three-dimensions on a two-dimensional surface is apparent in *The Oath of the Horatii* and *The Death of Socrates.*

The two paintings are *examples* to support the assertion that linear perspective is a major element in David's Neoclassicism.

Applying Logic

Logic, or sound reasoning, is the presentation of ideas in a clear and believable manner by avoiding *invalid premises* and *logical fallacies.* Being able to recognize sound reasoning allows the writer to construct persuasive theses and use support convincingly.

Invalid Premise

An *invalid premise* is an assumption erroneously applied to the conclusion.

Being a modernist, the poet Ezra Pound resisted classical influences.

The unstated premise—the basic assumption—behind this statement is the notion that *all modernists resist classical influences.* The reasoning is, therefore, that because Pound is a modernist, *he* resisted classical influences. Scholars do generally accept the notion that *most* modernists resist classical influences, but not that *all* modernists resist classical influences. This is a faulty conclusion, then, because it is based on a faulty unstated premise. The correct premise is that *most modernists resist classical influences.* Actually, Pound was heavily influenced by classical poetry. He is an exception to the general case.

Note: Students new to the humanities often make such assumptions. To avoid this problem, you should check your unstated assumptions to make sure that they are valid.

Logical Fallacies

A *logical fallacy* is a mistake in logic caused by misrepresenting evidence or distorting the issue. Most logical fallacies are based on faulty premises.

There are quite a number of logical fallacies. Only a few are offered here, but they should make you aware of and help you to avoid this kind of faulty reasoning.

• *Ad hominem* ("to the man") faults the person and avoids the issue at hand:

Emily Dickinson never travelled far from home, so her poetry can say little about human nature in general.

The perceived fault on Dickinson's part—a lack of travel—does not invalidate what she has to say about human nature. Dickinson's understanding of human nature should be considered through her poetry.

• *False authority* assumes that because someone is accomplished in one area, that person must be accomplished in another:

Georgia O'Keefe was a great painter of flowers, so she must have been a great botanist.

O'Keefe's ability to paint flowers in no way implies a knowledge of biochemical processes.

• *Hasty generalization* is an assertion made with too little evidence:

All Russian composers were fascinated with the Orient because so much Russian music uses Oriental motifs.

There were Russian composers who were not fascinated with the Orient, and much Russian music does not use Oriental motifs.

- *False dilemma* (or the *either/or* fallacy*)* assumes that there are only two choices when there are more than two:

An artist sees the world as seriously flawed or at least in need of improvement.

There is no reason to assume that an artist does not accept the world as is. You must at least consider other possibilities.

Critical Thinking and Critical Writing

The counterpart to critical thinking is "critical writing," or analytical writing. One may ponder a poem, a painting, a piece of music, or a philosophical idea in great depth and with great accuracy in one's own mind, but if those ideas are to be communicated precisely, then one must organize the argument on paper using detailed analysis, clear distinction between fact and opinion, adequate evidence, and consistent logic.

In preparation for writing, an analysis will naturally produce a series of observations expressed in thoughts that will be written down as sentences. Next, these ideas are organized into a hierarchy, a system of ideas organized according to importance in the context of the major idea, the thesis.

The *formal essay* is the structuring of these thoughts in an organized and consistent manner. The organization is structured into paragraphs that are controlled by a consistent design based on an overall sentence, *the thesis,* and secondary sentences, the *topic sentence* of each paragraph.

The first step in writing, after a thoughtful analysis, is to develop a working thesis.

Section 3

The First Step: The Thesis

· · · · · · · · · · · · · · · ·

The thesis is the main idea of the paper. Therefore, it should contain the major elements—the limited topic and the writer's opinion about the topic—and give the structure—the direction. You will want to develop a *working* thesis first.

You should begin to develop the thesis after you have done the analysis of your topic. While going over your class notes and reading notes that pertain to your topic—and studying the piece so you know it well—you should begin to write down your thoughts about the topic. When you feel that you have an idea of what you want to say, you should begin to develop the thesis by trying to write a clear sentence that explains your idea. This will be your working thesis, which may be refined as you progress through the outline and the writing.

Note: The quality of your thesis, and eventually your paper, will largely depend on how much time you spend thinking analytically about the topic.

Two sample theses and an explanation of their elements follow.

Sample Thesis One

Example One: A paper comparing Polykleitos's *Doryphorus* and Michelangelo's *David* by analyzing them as examples of classical works of art

Title: The *Doryphorus* and *David* as Classical Works

Introduction: define simplicity, balance, and perfection of form as criteria for classical art

Thesis: Polykleitos' *Doryphorus* and Michelangelo's *David* demonstrate the Classical aesthetic principles of simplicity, balance, and perfection of form.

Elements of the Thesis

Limited Topic: *Doryphorus*, *David*, and classical aesthetic principles

Writer's Position: the sculptures **do** demonstrate these principles

Direction: simplicity, balance, perfection of form

Topic Sentence for First Support Paragraph

Doryphorus and *David* demonstrate the classical principle of simplicity by the poses of the figures and . . .

Sample Thesis Two

Example Two: A paper exploring the influences of feudalism on the economic and social institutions of Europe

Title: The Influence of Feudalism on the Economic and Social Institutions of Europe

Introduction: define some of the terms concerning the major economic and social aspects of feudalism

Thesis: Feudalism developed economic and social institutions that affected European culture into the nineteenth century.

Elements of the Thesis

Limited Topic: feudalism's influence on economic and social institutions

Writer's Position: feudalism **did** affect economic and social institutions into the nineteenth century

Direction: effects on economic institutions and effects on social institutions

Topic Sentence for First Support Paragraph

The relations of production in the feudal system had a profound effect on the tenant-landlord relationship that developed . . .

Note: The broader direction in this thesis, the effects of feudalism on economic and social institutions, would break down into many more paragraphs, allowing for a much longer paper than the one suggested in example one.

Section 4

Sample Analysis: Poetry

The following analysis of a poem is meant to demonstrate the manner in which a piece of verbal art may be broken down into some of its formal elements in preparation for interpreting the content (meaning) and writing a formal essay. When analyzing works of art, you should keep your purpose clearly in mind. For instance, you may begin with the formal elements and work toward an interpretation of content—as will be done here. At other times, you may focus the analysis on formal elements alone or on a comparison of formal elements or content in two or more works of art.

An analysis of formal elements depends on the precise use of terminology. (See "Terms and Terminology" in Section 9, "Notes on Format and Style.") Therefore, understanding and applying the critical terms are essential for a successful paper. Many terms are employed for analyzing works of art, some specific to literature, music, or the visual arts. These critical terms and their definitions will be explained by your instructor and, of course, will be found in your humanities textbooks. Here, the relevant terms are given with the analysis.

An analysis of a poem, as with most works of art, is potentially infinite. You should analyze a work until you think that you have enough evidence to support a thesis and then begin the writing process. Otherwise, you may spend too much time analyzing and not enough time writing. You can always go back to the work for further evidence after you begin to formulate a thesis or even as you are writing the paper.

I Heard a Fly Buzz when I Died*

Emily Dickinson

I heard a fly buzz when I died;
    The stillness round my form
Was like the stillness in the air
    Between the heaves of storm.

The eyes beside had rung them dry,
    And breaths were gathering sure
For that last onset, when the king
    Be witnessed in his power.

> I willed my keepsakes, signed away
>> What portion of me I
> Could make assignable,—and then
>> There interposed a fly,
>
> With blue, uncertain, stumbling buzz,
>> Between the light and me;
> And then the windows failed, and then
>> I could not see to see.

Reading and Thinking

To discuss a work intelligently, you must know the elements that are in that work, so the analysis of any work of art depends on knowing the work well. A poem should be read closely several times, a painting or a sculpture should be observed thoroughly, and a piece of music should be listened to attentively and repeatedly. Next, you should think about the general subject of the work before you begin to direct the analysis.

In this poem, the lyric speaker (the "voice" of the poem) describes her own deathbed scene in which she is distracted at the point of death by the buzzing of a fly. Scenes of death are often associated with pain, suffering, and the settling of accounts, both worldly and spiritually. Many works of art about death are concerned with a divinity, an afterlife, or the lack of an afterlife. This is a first-person account of a death scene, so the attitude of the lyric speaker toward faith in a divinity and an afterlife, or a lack thereof, should be important.

The Title

The title is a good place to begin because titles often suggest possible analytical approaches. Here the first line is given as the title, and "I Heard a Fly Buzz when I Died" suggests three motifs: sense perception ("I heard"), death ("when I died"), and the "buzzing fly." The recurring *image* of the "buzzing fly" is the only recurring word motif in the poem, so this should be a point of emphasis in the analysis.

(*Image,* a most important word in poetic discussion, usually refers to an element created by the poetic use of language. See "Diction" later in this section.)

Criteria for Analysis

The elements that you choose to analyze should be the elements that are most striking in the work itself, and here *motif, diction, setting,* and *symbol* will be employed because the poem contains clear examples of these.

Motifs

A *motif* is a formal element—image, word, object, phrase, action, incident, or device—that recurs in a work. For instance, a motif in music is the shortest intelligible melodic or rhythmic figure, maybe four or five notes, whereas in literature a motif could be "the evil stepmother," or a constant reference to "the passing of time," or "death" as in this poem. The term *motif* has a broad application, sometimes referring to elements that recur in a single work, sometimes referring to elements that recur in art or literature in general.

These are some motifs in Dickinson's poem and their examples:

Motif	Examples
Death	"died," "last onset," "willed my keepsakes," "I could not see"
Sense perception	"heard," "buzz," "stillness," "eyes," "breaths," "light," "see"
Buzzing fly	"fly buzz," "fly," "buzz" (the only recurring words)

This list does not exhaust the number of motifs and their examples. However, this should be enough to formulate a preliminary idea of the subject of the poem. The poem appears to be about death, sense perception, and a "buzzing fly."

Setting

The *setting* presents the lyric speaker dying in a room, lying on a bed, and noticing a "buzzing fly." The assumption is made here on the evidence of "when I died," "stillness round my form," and the "buzzing fly."

Diction

Diction is the choice of words, phrases, and *figures* in a work of literature. A poem's diction can be, for instance, either *figurative* or *literal,* which will be used here. Other criteria for diction might be *abstract* or *concrete, colloquial* or *formal.*

In the first line of this poem, Dickinson uses figurative language: "The stillness round my form / Was like the stillness in the air / Between the heaves of storm." This is not a strictly *denotative* or literal use of language. Instead, these lines offer *connotations* (the secondary significances and feelings of a word) that suggest a meaning beyond the purely descriptive. This is *figurative* language.

A *figure* is a deviation in language from ordinary usage. Several of the most common figures are *simile, metaphor, synesthesia,* and *personification.* Figures are used to create connotation and ambiguity (more than one meaning) in words so that poems can mean more than the literal sense of the words themselves. In an analysis of figurative language, you should begin on a more literal level and move toward a meaning beyond the literal.

A *simile* is a comparison of two things using "like" or "as."

Simile: "The stillness round my form / Was like the stillness in the air / Between the heaves of a storm."

In the first stanza, Dickinson compares the lull or calm around the "form" in the room (the dying body) with the lull or calm between the violent activity of a storm, but the *meaning* of that comparison is left open to interpretation. This comparison could mean that the dying body is experiencing fits of violent physical pain or that the dying person is experiencing fits of mental anguish over death, both suggested by "the heaves of storm." This offers interpretation on two levels: a literal level (physical pain) and a symbolic level (mental anguish).

A *metaphor* is a comparison of two things without "like" or "as."

Metaphor: "And then the windows failed."

The most common *metaphor* directly states a comparison of two things: *He was a lion in war.* The fourth stanza of this poem gives an *implicit metaphor.* The metaphor implies that there is a comparison but leaves out one part. Windows do not "fail," but human beings fail, so the implied missing part of the comparison is the lyric speaker. The following line says, "I could not see to see," so the metaphor implies that the failure of the windows is associated with the failure of the dying person's sight. Once again, two levels are suggested. On the one hand, the dying lyric speaker's vision fails physically at the point of death. On the other hand, words such as "window" and "see" have traditionally been associated in literature with an inner vision of knowledge, and "light" has often been associated with faith. This association is reinforced by the "could not see to see." The doubling of "see" clearly implies sight beyond the physical senses. Therefore, the image of the failure of sight could be understood as a failure of knowledge or faith on the part of the lyric speaker.

Synesthesia is a figure created when a word usually associated with one sense is associated with another.

Synesthesia: "There interposed a fly, / With blue, uncertain, stumbling buzz,"

A "blue [. . .] buzz" demonstrates s*ynesthesia* when one word (blue) usually associated with one sense (sight) is associated with another sense (sound). This line occurs in the fourth stanza when the lyric speaker suffers a failure of sight. Therefore, the s*ynesthesia* reinforces the confusion and failure of the senses at the point of death on the physical, or literal, level and on the higher level. At the point of death, the lyric speaker is unable to "see" anything either physically or spiritually.

Personification is to give human attributes and feelings to inanimate objects or abstract concepts.

Personification: "With blue, uncertain, stumbling buzz,
  Between the light [. . .];
  And then the windows failed, [. . .] "

"Stumbling" and "uncertain" are not commonly associated with a "buzz" but rather with the inability to walk confidently and properly, and windows may "fail to open," but "failure" is usually applied to human intentions. These two lines from the fourth stanza demonstrate *personification* by associating the confusion and failure of the human senses with the objects of perception themselves. As was the case with the preceding figures, the *personification* also suggests the possibility of interpretation on two levels, a failure to see the fly properly and an inability to see through the window beyond, possibly to the spiritual.

The figurative language of the poem allows a meaning on two levels. On the literal level, the poem is about the lyric speaker's physical death. The figurative language, however, suggests that the poem is also about the failure to "see to see" "the light," a failure of faith.

Symbol

A *symbol* in literary analysis is a word or phrase that represents an object, an event, or something else, which in turn signifies something beyond itself. Finding a symbol in a literary work is a matter of locating a word or a phrase that the author emphasizes and then interpreting the symbol in the context of the entire poem. Like figurative language, a symbol must be interpreted on two levels: the literal and the symbolic.

The "buzzing fly" is emphasized as the only distinctly recurring image of the poem. The word "fly" and "buzz" occur in the first line, and they carry over from the third stanza to the fourth and concluding stanza, thus giving them points of emphasis. Finally, the relatively calm setting of the death scene seems to be interrupted when the "buzzing fly" is "interposed" "between the light and me," thus initiating the *synesthesia* and the failure of the lyric speaker's sight at the point of death.

On the symbolic level, the connotations of the symbol are taken into consideration. A "buzzing fly" is usually associated with irritation and distraction, something that is annoying, and the fly is interposed in the poem "between the light and me." The fly interferes with the seeing of the light, so this could be understood as an inability to know with finality if death holds an afterlife or the inability to see the spiritual because of the distractions of life. In this sense, the poem contemplates faith, the "buzzing fly" being a symbol of the difficulty of faith.

Special Details

A major point of the analysis should be to note any striking details that may fail to be taken into account while analyzing the elements that you have chosen. In Dickinson's poem, two striking details have not yet been considered: the image of the king and the curious fact that the lyric speaker is dead yet is speaking the poem.

The image of the king is the only reference to anything exclusively outside the setting of the poem itself. All other references may be accounted for in the poem itself and on a literal level. Therefore, the "king" must be interpreted on a symbolic level. In much western poetry since biblical times, "king" has been associated with God, and the reference here suggests God, but the reference is ambiguous. "Be witnessed" leaves in doubt *who* will witness his power. "That last onset, when the king / Be witnessed in his power" could suggest that the "king" (God) will be seen after death in his power by the lyric speaker or that death itself, the natural act of dying, will witness (certify) his power, in which case the "king" may represent the power of death over life and not God. To decide with certainty is impossible because evidence in the poem cannot decide this issue.

The second special detail, the fact that the lyric speaker is speaking in the past tense about her own death, is a *paradox* (a contradictory statement that may be true). Working out a paradox is a difficult task, but usually is a major interpretive point. "I heard a fly buzz when I died" is a paradox because one cannot speak in the past tense about one's own death. Once again, an interpretation on a symbolic level is required. Either the lyric speaker is speaking from the afterlife, or the lyric speaker is merely contemplating death in the past tense for some effect. No one speaks "from the grave" and can be heard in this world, and there is no evidence in the poem itself to suggest that the speaker is only contemplating death in the past tense for effect. Therefore, this paradox creates a deep ambiguity that may be connected to the ambiguity of "the king."

The analysis to this point has established that the poem may be understood on two levels: the physical (literal) death of the lyric speaker and her difficulty of realizing faith ("I could not see to see"). Because the reference to the "king" remains ambiguous and the lyric speaker's use of the past tense is a paradox, they may represent the paradox and difficulty of faith. That is, *faith is precisely difficult because it requires an absolute belief in something that cannot be known absolutely.* Finally, as has already been established, the symbol of the "buzzing fly" represents this difficulty of faith.

From Analysis to Thesis

Formulating your thesis from the analysis moves in the opposite direction as the analysis. The analysis collects information to arrive at an interpretation. To formulate your thesis, you begin with your conclusion (interpretation) and collect the evidence to support that conclusion from the analysis. You will usually have information and ideas about the poem that you will not use in your paper. You will only need to use the evidence that is necessary to support your thesis.

Because the purpose of analyzing Dickinson's poem was to arrive at a meaning (the content embodied in the formal elements), the content here is in the form of a *theme*.

A *theme* is the meaning, or "message," that the artist or author has to say about human life in general expressed in the work of art.

The conclusion of the analysis can be seen as the theme of the poem:

> Faith is difficult because it requires an absolute belief in something that cannot be known absolutely.

At this point, you should formulate a thesis. To do this, you will want to rephrase or even simplify the theme so that you can use it in your thesis statement. The introduction and the body of the paper will allow you to give all the necessary explanation.

> Dickinson's poem, "I Heard a Fly Buzz when I Died," contemplates the difficulty of faith . . .

This represents the *limited subject* and *the writer's position.*

> **Limited Subject:** "I Heard a Fly Buzz" and the difficulty of faith

> **Writer's Position:** Dickinson's poem **does** contemplate the difficulty of faith.

The final part of the thesis, *the support,* will be the general categories that you choose to back up your position. To decide what support you will use, you need to review your analysis. The major points of support in this analysis are the figurative language, the symbol of the "buzzing fly," and two special details.

When you add the support to the thesis statement, you will want to use proper terminology. It may take some time to work out the proper terminology, but this is necessary for the clarity of your thesis and argument. The terms "figurative language" and "symbol" are recognized terms, but "special details" is not precise poetic terminology. Ambiguity is the important aspect of both of the special details, so this term will give the thesis clarity.

> Dickinson's "I Heard a Fly Buzz when I Died" contemplates the difficulty of faith through figurative language, the symbol of the buzzing fly, and ambiguity.

Note: Often the limited topic itself will serve as a title:

> Dickinson's "I Heard a Fly Buzz when I Died" and the Difficulty of Faith

From Thesis to Outline

After you have formulated the thesis, the outline should follow. You use the outline primarily to organize the support into a good structure. (See Section 6, "Preparing the Structure: The Outline.") The following is the beginning of an outline for this paper.

Title: Dickinson's "I Heard a Fly Buzz when I Died" and the Difficulty of Faith

Introduction: A definition of faith as difficult because one cannot have knowledge of the afterlife in this life and Dickinson's ability to present this difficulty of faith in poetic language

Thesis: Dickinson's "I Heard a Fly Buzz when I Died" contemplates the difficulty of faith through figurative language, the symbol of the buzzing fly, and ambiguity.

Support Paragraph #1

Topic Sentence: The simile in the first stanza, "The stillness round my form / Was like the stillness in the air / Between the heaves of storm," introduces the two levels upon which the poem may be interpreted by suggesting both physical and mental anguish.

Support Paragraph #2

Topic Sentence: In the fourth stanza, the implicit metaphor, "And then the windows failed," and the redundant phrase, "I could not see to see," can be understood figuratively to represent the difficulty of faith.

After you have written working topic sentences for all or most of your paragraphs, you will organize your support under each topic sentence in preparation for developing the paragraphs and creating the transitions between them.

Now you are ready to write the first draft. This is the manner in which an analysis is organized into a formal essay.

Section 5

Sample Analysis: Painting

The following analysis breaks down a work of art into its formal elements. The purpose is to classify the work as representative of a certain style and period in a formal essay. As in any analysis, you should keep your purpose clearly in mind. In this case, you will begin with the formal elements and work toward demonstrating that the work meets the criteria for that style and, ultimately, to see the work of art as representing the values of a certain cultural period.

One major purpose of studying the visual arts is to make the student aware of the techniques employed by artists so that the student may have a deeper appreciation of the works themselves. Another is to allow the student to understand those techniques as the expression of the intellectual concerns of a given period.

The example here will be Jacques-Louis David's *The Oath of The Horatii,* a representative work of Neoclassicism and the Enlightenment.

With a piece of visual art, the analysis begins with the division into form (structure) and content. You will become familiar with the terminology relevant to the form and content of painting and to specific styles in class and from your textbooks. For the sake of discussion here, the terminology will be given and then applied to David's work. As with poetry or any other work of art, the elements chosen for the analysis should depend on two factors: you should choose elements that are clearly apparent in the work, and you should choose enough elements to support the thesis of your paper.

Form

In painting, the form may be seen as the *composition* achieved through certain *techniques* and demonstrating certain *aesthetic values.* These techniques and aesthetic values are the criteria by which a work is judged as representative of a style.

- *Composition:* The arrangement of visual elements
- *Technique:* A systematic procedure by which an artistic aim is accomplished such as the composition itself
- *Aesthetic value:* A quality considered by a period (style) to be an attribute of "beauty"

Aesthetics is a broad category. For instance, nineteenth-century Realism considered the representation of human faults and even physical deformities

Jacques-Louis David, *Oath of the Horatii,* 1784.
Used by permission of Reunion des Musees Nationaux, Paris/Art Resource, New York.

to be artistically "beautiful," associating the beautiful with "true to life," whereas Classicism considered the creation of the perfect form by eliminating human faults and deformities to be "the beautiful." Aesthetic values not only reveal a period's sense of "the beautiful" but also the beliefs and attitudes of the culture.

Classicism is the style of the art and literature of ancient Greece and Rome. The values and forms of Classicism have been the major influence on the art and literature of the western tradition and were directly emulated during the Renaissance and the Enlightenment (the period of Neoclassicism in art). The values of Classicism to be analyzed here are *balance, simplicity, restraint,* and *perfection of form.* These criteria are not exhaustive, but they are major values that allow the painting to be classified according to style.

Other traditions, such as those of Chinese, Buddhist, African, or any other culture, have their own artistic techniques and aesthetic values. Works of art from these cultures should be analyzed and evaluated according to the dictates of their own traditions. Analyses that compare works from different cultures should first evaluate each work relative to its own tradition and then compare the traditions. In other words, to evaluate a work by the eighteenth-century Chinese artist, Lang Shih-ning, done on paper in ink and color, according to the techniques and values of western neoclassical oil painting would reveal little about the art or culture of eighteenth-century China. However, a comparison of the different techniques by which Lang Shih-ning and David achieved perspective in their respective works could reveal insights into the differences (and possible similarities) of art and culture between eighteenth-century Europe and eighteenth-century China.

Neoclassical Values

- *Balance:* The preference for arranging the visual elements so that any major element on one side of the composition is complemented by a major element on the other side of the composition

- *Simplicity:* The preference for a clear and easily comprehensible composition; the avoidance of complexity; the avoidance of nonessential detail and ornamentation

- *Restraint:* The preference for control and poise, both emotionally and visually

- *Perfection of Form:* The preference for proportionally and mathematically flawless forms; the "lifelike" represented as perfect

- *Linear Perspective:* A technique to create the illusion of three-dimensional space on a two-dimensional surface through the convergence of lines to a vanishing point on the horizon line

Content

Subject Matter

The event, story, person, or thing that the work represents is the *subject matter*. The subject of a painting in the western tradition has usually been considered as a *narrative*. Even portraits imply the life and accomplishments of the subject. As a result, paintings have been traditionally interpreted by "reading" them to locate a story or a *theme*. *Modernism* of the early twentieth century introduced *abstract* or *nonrepresentational* art (that does not represent observable aspects of nature) and has altered the tradition in this respect, but before Modernism, the interpretation of *narrative* in works of art was the rule.

Cultural Context

Works of art are usually studied in their *cultural context*. That is, they are seen as expressing the ideals, aspirations, and values of a given age or period: ancient Greece and Rome (the Classical World), the Middle Ages, the Renaissance, the Reformation (Mannerism), the Baroque Age, the Enlightenment, the Romantic Period, the Industrial Revolution and nineteenth-century Realism, the Age of Modernism. These designations are fluid, meaning they are not always applied consistently and precisely, but you need to be aware of the general characteristics of these periods and their styles to understand the cultural significance of a given work of art. One major goal of studying the humanities is a deeper understanding of the values of different cultures and periods.

Theme

The *theme* is the meaning of the work, the idea that the artist presents concerning human life in general. The theme is often considered to reflect the cultural values of the given period.

Form Analysis

After having understood some of the major formal elements of Neoclassicism, close observation of the work itself will reveal the evidence to support David's *Oath of the Horatii* as representative of that style.

Linear Perspective

David's use of linear perspective is seen most clearly in the paving stones and the vanishing point, located behind the central figure's grasp of the swords. The lines between paving stones converge at an unseen vanishing point that would correspond to the horizon line beyond the far wall of the building. The vanishing point is further emphasized by being located directly behind the central figure's grasp of the swords. The vanishing point, therefore, becomes the point around which the composition is organized. The visual elements are mathematically situated in three-dimensional space according to the vanishing point.

Balance

The balance is achieved in the composition by positioning three major figures on each side of the central figure.

Simplicity

The composition is clear and easily comprehensible. The seven major figures are plainly grouped and stand out distinctively, and the lack of furniture, wall ornamentation, or other nonessential details places attention directly on the figures.

Restraint

The composition is controlled by the poses of the figures. The repetition of the stances of the figures on the left controls the emotion of the "oath," and the "lamenting" figures on the right lack wild gesticulations or other overt displays of emotion.

Perfection of Form

The legs and arms of the figures as well as their height show no flaws or individuality in form. They are created according to a *canon* (the classical ideal proportions for representation of the human figure).

The formal elements classify David's work in the *style* of Neoclassicism.

Content Analysis

Subject Matter

The subject of the painting comes from the history of the early Roman Republic. The Horatii were a leading family in Rome, and one of the sisters had fallen in love with one of Rome's enemies, a member of the Curiatii family of Alba Longa. The painting captures the moment when the Horatii brothers take an oath to defend Rome at all costs.

The narrative of the painting concerns the oath of allegiance to the Roman state by the Horatii brothers, which leads to the death of one Horatii sister.

During combat in which all three of the Curiatii brothers are killed, two Horatii brothers die. On his way home from battle, the surviving brother meets his "disloyal" sister, weeping over the Curiatii brother whom she was to marry. Seeing this as disloyalty to Rome, he stabs her to death. Enlightenment thinking would understand this situation as a struggle between the values of the past and the values of the new and emerging society: loyalty to the state takes precedence over loyalty to the family.

Cultural Context

The *philosophes* (French for "philosophers"), who were the leaders of intellectual thought during the Enlightenment, were much concerned with the idea of a rational state based on liberty and equality. In general, they believed that traditional society, or the *ancien régime*—in which aristocratic families held privileged positions—was based in religious superstition and depended on the ignorance of common people. A major goal of the Enlightenment was, therefore, to educate the common people to free them from superstition and make them participatory citizens in a rational state based on liberty and equality. Thus, reason was held superior to the emotional appeal of religion, family, and other traditional social ties. This championing of human reason accounts as well for the highly ordered and rational composition of neoclassical painting.

The *philosophes* considered the ancient democracy and republicanism of Greece and Rome as examples of rational states. As a result, they looked to the ancients for inspiration not only in politics but also in literature, architecture, and the visual arts.

David's painting clearly reflects the ideals of the Enlightenment by emulating classical aesthetic values and championing loyalty and duty to the state over the demands of family. In other words, for the Enlightenment, the oath of the Horatii would symbolize loyalty to the rationally founded state whereas family loyalty would represent the values of the *ancien régime*.

Theme

The theme of David's *Oath of the Horatii* could be stated as "loyalty to the state requires the sacrifice of traditional loyalties." Thus, the content of David's work is representative of the *period* of the Enlightenment.

From Analysis to Thesis

After reviewing the analysis, the major elements of form and content must be organized into a thesis that classifies David's painting as a work of Neoclassicism and the Enlightenment.

- *Form:* balance, simplicity, restraint, perfection of form, linear perspective, special detail
- *Content:* subject matter, cultural context, theme

The purpose of the paper is to demonstrate that *The Oath of the Horatii* is a work of Neoclassicism that reflects Enlightenment values. Therefore, the limited topic and the writer's position should reflect this idea.

Limited Topic: *The Oath of the Horatii,* Neoclassicism and the Enlightenment

Writer's Position: *The Oath of the Horatii* **is** a work of Neoclassicism and the Enlightenment

The direction is the evidence that will support this assertion. However, to use all the direction in the thesis itself would be far too cumbersome:

Jacques-Louis David's *Oath of the Horatii* demonstrates Neoclassicism and Enlightenment values in its balance, simplicity, restraint, perfection of form, linear perspective, special detail, subject matter, cultural context, and theme.

In this case, you can simplify the direction into "form" and "content":

Jacques-Louis David's *Oath of the Horatii* demonstrates Neoclassicism and Enlightenment values in form and content.

From this thesis, you will be able to break down the form and content into the various elements in the topic sentences.

From Thesis to Outline

Introduction

You could take several approaches to introduce your thesis. For instance, you could briefly explain the relationship between form and content in neoclassical art: the ordered and rational techniques used for composition are a reflection of the Enlightenment's championing of reason. You could also explain that David's work in general demonstrates ordered and rational composition. You might, on the other hand, briefly discuss the theme and suggest that the Enlightenment ideal of a rational state corresponds to the ideal form in Neoclassicism. Another possibility would be to save the decision on the introduction until you have worked out the structure of the paper.

Thesis

After you have introduced the limited topic, you should state the thesis at the end of the first paragraph.

Thesis: Jacques-Louis David's *Oath of the Horatii* demonstrates Neoclassicism and Enlightenment values in form and content.

Topic Sentence

The first topic sentence will relate to the first element of the direction of the thesis, Neoclassicism.

First Topic Sentence: The composition of David's painting is balanced, simple, and restrained.

The development of the paragraph will give the evidence to support the topic sentence by briefly describing the elements in the composition that correspond to these principles.

Transition Sentence

The transition sentence between the first and second support paragraphs connects the two by referring to the first element of the direction, Neoclassicism, and then introducing the topic of the next paragraph, the design and figures.

Transition Sentence: Neoclassicism is further demonstrated in the design and figures.

Second Topic Sentence: The design of the painting is based on linear perspective, and the figures reflect neoclassical perfection.

Referring back to the thesis and forward to the next paragraph, transition sentences give the formal essay good coherence by connecting major ideas.

Topic and Transition Sentences

The remainder of the outline will consist of topic and transition sentences. These are most important because the coherence of the paper depends on the thought connections between paragraphs

Transition Sentence: The **rational and classical form** of David's painting reflects the **values of the Enlightenment.**

Third Topic Sentence: The concern with **order and rationality** demonstrated in the composition is matched in the **subject matter and theme.**

Transition Sentence: This **theme** clearly identifies the work with the **ideals of the Enlightenment.**

Fourth Topic Sentence: The **form and content** of David's *The Oath of the Horatii* make it an excellent example of **Neoclassicism and the ideals of the Enlightenment.**

When you repeat key terms in the thesis, topic sentences and transition sentences in your outline, you will be able to clearly see the argument develop. When the outline is complete, you are ready to add the support and develop the individual paragraphs. The following section discusses the outline in detail.

·················

Section 6

Preparing the Structure: The Outline

·················

Students rarely enjoy doing an outline for a paper; nevertheless, a good outline will help you organize your thoughts and save time writing. Without an outline, you may find yourself repeating points or otherwise losing the focus of your thesis. A good outline allows you to lay out the structure of your paper according to the direction of your thesis. In doing so, you will be able to see how the ideas connect. This will allow you to construct good topic sentences and make transitions between paragraphs.

The outline is based on your thesis as it is broken down into paragraphs. Each section of the outline should correspond to a paragraph of your paper. The first sentence should be your topic sentence followed by your support sentences, and the section should end with your transition sentence. The outline is a "working" project; that is, while making the outline, you begin to put your thoughts into complete sentences and begin to see how the sentences connect so that your paragraphs in the final version will have unity and coherence. During this process, you will often move pieces of evidence, sentences, and ideas around to see where they are most effective.

The first step is to develop working topic sentences so that you can determine how many paragraphs you will have and in which order you will arrange them. Next, you may begin to arrange evidence, terms, phrases, and even some full sentences into the paragraph in which you believe they will be used.

Paragraph #1

Depending on length, the introduction could be more than one paragraph.
Introduction (possible ways to introduce the thesis):

1. The historical, literary, social, or artistic context of the thesis may be described.

2. The definitions of key terms can often introduce the thesis as well as establish terminology to be used throughout the paper.

3. Special information needed to understand the thesis may be used.

4. Often giving names of authors, artists, characters, titles to be discussed and why they are relevant is effective.

Avoid overly general introductions, such as sweeping statements about life in general or statements so obvious as to be meaningless. As always is the case, be as specific as possible.

Thesis (should come as the final sentence of the introduction): The thesis is a one-sentence statement including limited topic, writer's position, and direction.

In a very long paper, the thesis may take more than one sentence; however, it is always best to make the thesis statement in one sentence no matter how long the paper because the thesis controls the structure of the paper and your thinking about the topic. In other words, you do not have good control over the material until you can explain it clearly in one sentence.

Paragraph #2

In general, all support paragraphs should include the following:

1. The topic sentence should directly support the thesis and correspond to the first element of the direction.

2. The support material for the topic sentence consists of the evidence—facts, quotes, paraphrases from secondary sources, and other relevant material.

3. The development of the paragraph is an explanation of the connection between the topic sentence, the support material, and the thesis.

4. The transition sentence connecting the major point of one paragraph to the topic sentence of the next paragraph gives coherence between paragraphs.

Paragraph #3, #4, #5, and all succeeding paragraphs are support paragraphs similar in structure to paragraph #2.

Conclusion

1. If the paper is long, a restatement or paraphrase of the thesis may be necessary; however, in a short paper, a restatement of the thesis usually sounds repetitious.

2. A good way to conclude a paper, whether long or short, is to suggest a significance for the thesis that places it in a larger context by placing the thesis in relation to other ideas about or positions on the subject.

·················

Section 7

Preparing the Final Product: The Format

·················

After you have written your paper, you are ready to prepare the format before submitting your work. This is an important step because a neat and correct format will usually predispose your instructor favorably toward your paper. *Note:* These format guidelines for academic papers follow the MLA style, and an example in this style follows.

- **Margins:** Papers should observe a one-inch margin on the top, bottom, and sides of each page.

- **Heading:** The heading should appear in the upper left-hand corner and be double spaced.

- **Title:** The title should be double spaced below the heading and double spaced above the first line of text. (See Section 9, "Notes on Format and Style" for punctuation of paper titles.)

- **Text:** The text of the paper is the actual physical body of the paper, the lines organized into paragraphs.

- **First Line:** The first line of text should be indented one-half inch.

- **Double Spacing:** Academic papers should always be double spaced.

- **Right Margin:** Paragraphs should never be "justified"; the right margin should be "ragged."

- **Indentation:** The first line of each paragraph is indented one-half inch.

- **Page Numbers (Header):** Beginning on the first page, your last name and the page number should appear in the upper right-hand corner. The number should appear to the right of the name, and this header is placed one-half inch from the top and one inch from the right edge. Beginning on the second page, there is a double space before the first line of text. To set the header, you may choose the "header/footer" option on your word processing program.

- **Cover Pages:** In general, cover pages should not be used unless requested by the instructor.

- **Binding:** Usually, one staple in the upper left-hand corner is appropriate. However, you should consult the instructor on this matter.

Note: Papers written for the humanities are usually indented. However, a block format could also be used in which there is a triple space between paragraphs but no paragraph indentation. As in all college papers, lines are double spaced in this style as well.

· · · · · · · · · · · · · · · ·

Section 8

Sample Paper in the MLA Style

· · · · · · · · · · · · · · ·

[one inch]

[one-half inch]
Jourjy 1

Jasmine Jourjy   [double-space]

HUM 2243–001

Dr. Milam

April 23, 2001

[double-space]
The Ideology of the Bourgeoisie

during the Eighteenth-Century Enlightenment
[double-space]

[indent one-half inch]

[one inch]

The rise of the bourgeois class intensified during the eighteenth-century
[double-space]
Enlightenment, an era in which the equality and improvement of humanity were

[one inch]

major concerns. The bourgeoisie—a merchant, capitalist, and industrial class—

professed the ideas of laissez-faire capitalism and political liberalism, major ide-

ologies developed in the context of the Enlightenment's concern with the

betterment of humanity. Political liberalism emphasizes equality and the natural

rights of man. "Laissez-faire" means "let alone"; thus, laissez-faire capitalism

promotes an economic market that operates without the intervention of govern-

ment regulation or control. Laissez-faire capitalism and political liberalism were

ideologies of the rising bourgeoisie because these ideas justified revolutionary

economic change, equality in politics and society, and merit over privilege as the

basis for social and economic success.

Laissez-faire capitalism represented a revolutionary change in the econ-

omy by challenging and eventually replacing the mercantile system. Adam

[one inch]

30

[one inch]

[double-space]

[one inch]

Smith's *The Wealth of Nations* introduced and explained the theoretical basis of laissez-faire capitalism and the advantages of the free market. Historically, laissez-faire capitalism was a reaction against the monarchy's absolute control over the economy, which included the creation of state monopolies, regulation of imports and exports, and heavy taxes. One of Smith's key ideas is "the invisible hand of the market." Within a given market, he maintained, supply and demand would tend toward equilibrium and raise the standard of living of all citizens as long as the government refrained from intervention. The idea furthered the cause of the bourgeoisie to exclude the government for their own benefit. Ultimately, the gradual change from mercantilism to laissez-faire capitalism over the course of the nineteenth century justified the bourgeoisie's claim to power and assertion of control over economic and social matters.

[one inch]

While the economic rise of the bourgeoisie was justified through the ideology of laissez-faire capitalism, political liberalism helped to justify the rise of the bourgeois class in politics and society. Political liberalism focuses on the equality of man, stating that all men are equal according to natural law. This idea was necessary in order for the bourgeoisie to rival the aristocracy in political and social affairs. The English philosopher John Locke formulated the natural rights of man, the creed of political liberalism. Locke claimed that all men had an equal right to life, liberty and property in law. In other words, government, aristocracy, or any other agency had no right to arbitrarily deny these rights without due process of law. In the latter eighteenth and the early nineteenth centuries, these

[one inch]

[one inch]

[double-space]

[one inch]

[one inch]

core ideas came to form the basis of the rights of citizens in the western democra-

cies, demonstrating the political dominance of the bourgeoisie.

Following from the ideas of the equality and the natural rights of citizens, another central idea of political liberalism concerns the basis for social, political and economic advancement. The aristocratic society that dominated European culture in the eighteenth century was based upon aristocratic privilege; that is, positions in government, economy, and society were granted according to social rank. Of course, nearly all important positions were given to aristocrats. If citizens were to have equal rights and opportunity, then aristocratic privilege had to give way. Political liberalism, then, advocated the individual's merit—the education, abilities, and achievements—as the basis for social, political, and economic advancement and reward. Finally, bourgeois ideology claimed that society as a whole would become more prosperous under such a system because the best abilities of the nation would be put to use. At least theoretically, the concept of merit over privilege allowed the bourgeoisie to compete with the aristocracy, and gradually through the nineteenth century, the bourgeoisie began to gain equality in economics, politics, and society.

The eighteenth-century Enlightenment saw the theoretical formulation of the bourgeois ideology of laissez-faire capitalism and political liberalism. These ideas backed the rise of the bourgeoisie as a class in economic, political, and social affairs, justifying the wide gains that the class made during the nineteenth century when the bourgeoisie came to dominance. Eventually, laissez-faire capitalism and political liberalism became major elements of the cultural tradition of the West.

[one inch]

Part Two

Writing and Research Basics

. . . .

Section 9

Notes on Format and Style

. . . .

Format

The following notes refer to major matters that you need to know in preparing the format, and they refer to points of style. For punctuation, the MLA style is followed.

Fonts

You should use a twelve-point font and a standard style such as Times Roman or Courier and avoid odd or striking font styles. You should use always use black ink.

Headers

You should not use a cover page unless the instructor requests one. Instead, your name, the course number, the instructor's name, and the date of submission should appear in the upper left-hand corner, one inch from the top and one inch from the left edge of the paper. (See Section 8, "Sample Paper in the MLA Style.")

Title

The title of the paper should appear as follows:

Classical Values in Pound's *Cantos*

The title of a paper is never underlined or put in quotation marks, bold, or a larger font size than the text itself. All major words are capitalized, and other titles within the paper title are appropriately punctuated. (For example, the title of a poem is placed in quotation marks, or the title of a painting is placed

in italics or underlined.) Major words are all words except articles, preposi-
tions, coordinating conjunctions, and the "to" in infinitives.

The title should always be centered and double spaced down from the
heading, and there should be a double space before the first line of text.

Paragraph Format

The first line of each paragraph should be indented one-half inch, and all text
should be double spaced.

Page Numbers

Pages should be numbered by placing your last name and the page number
in the upper-right corner of the page, one-half inch from the top and one inch
from the right edge of the paper.

Style

Title

The title of the paper should reflect the specific content of the paper; that is,
it should never be simply the name of the subject but, rather, should suggest
the purpose—what the paper plans to demonstrate.

An Analysis of Poetic Image in Apollinaire's *Alcools*

The Classical Idea of Simplicity in the Parthenon

The Social Position of the Peasant on the Medieval Manor

An Analysis of Strindberg's *Madam Julie* according
to Aristotle's Elements of Tragedy

Tense

When writing about events that take place in fiction, drama, or any other
imaginative literature, you should use the present tense. With historical
events, because they actually took place, the past tense is proper.

Rashkolnikov, Dostoevsky's hero in *Crime and Punishment,* **tries** to escape his
conscience throughout the course of the novel.

Dostoevsky **was** a notorious gambler.

In Shakespeare's play, Othello **is** dominated by jealousy.

Julius Caesar **defeated** the Gauls and **wrote** about his conquest.

When discussing relative events in a work of fiction, time designators are used.

After Macbeth *kills* the king, he *talks* to Lady Macbeth.

Tone

You should not "lead" the reader; that is, you should not tell the reader what the paper will do:

> This paper will examine Macbeth's motives . . .

Instead, you should directly state the matter at hand and simply write about the subject.

> Macbeth's motives are ambition, pride, . . .

Naming the Subject Early

The name of the works and the artists, writers, or historical figures considered in the paper should always be named in the first paragraph, preferably as soon as possible. The first line of your paper may look like this.

> Working for the *polis* of Athens, Kallikrates and Iktinos designed the Parthenon that was constructed between 447 and 438 BC.

Use of Names

When referring to artists, writers, or historical figures, the first and last name should be used on first reference, then only the last name on all subsequent references (unless tradition dictates otherwise: Napoleon, Michelangelo, Leonardo, for instance, are referred to by their first names):

> **Leo Tolstoy** experienced immense fame and fortune as a young man. His career was extremely long and his works prolific. Eventually, **Tolstoy** became the "conscience" of Russia.

> **Leonardo da Vinci** was a prodigy, surpassing his master and achieving excellence at an early age. Eventually, **Leonardo** would paint *Mona Lisa,* widely considered to be one of the greatest paintings of all time.

Punctuating Quotations

Direct quotations used from a source are placed in quotation marks and introduced by a colon if the quotation is introduced by a full sentence. However, if the quotation is a part of the sentence structure, a comma or no punctuation should be used.

> Referring to Homais, Flaubert sums up the triumph of the pettiness of French provincial life in the final line of the novel: "He has just been given the Legion of Honor" (255).

> Summing up Onegin's thoughts, Pushkin says, "Such were the young rake's meditations" (13).

> Chopin describes Mrs. Mallard as "afflicted with a heart trouble" (171).

Punctuation with Quotations

In the text, commas and periods are placed within quotation marks, but colons and semicolons are placed outside.

> Stevens does this in "Sunday Morning," and he repeats it in "The Man with the Blue Guitar."

> Maupassant uses the technique in "The Jewels"; the other elements are completely lacking.

Punctuating Quotations of Poetry

When punctuating poetry in quotations, there are two considerations. If the quotation is three lines or less of the text (or two lines according to the Chicago style), a slash (/) should be employed between the lines of the original.

> **Original:** To be, or not to be—that is the question:
> Whether 'tis nobler in the mind to suffer
> The slings and arrows of outrageous fortune,
> Or to take up arms . . .

> **Quotation:** Then Shakespeare's Hamlet makes his famous soliloquy: "To be or not to be—that is the question: / Whether 'tis nobler in the mind to suffer / The slings and arrows of outrageous fortune, / Or to take up arms [. . .]" (*Ham.* 3.1. 56–63).

If the quotation is more than three lines of text, the poetry should be indented one inch from the left margin and double spaced (unless the poem employs unusual spacing). When quotations are set off from the text, quotation marks are not used, and a full colon introduces the quotation.

> Then Shakespeare's Hamlet makes his famous soliloquy:

> To be, or not to be—that is the question:
> Whether 'tis nobler in the mind to suffer
> The slings and arrows of outrageous fortune,
> Or to take up arms against a sea of troubles,
> And by opposing, end them. To die, to sleep—
> No more, and by a sleep to say we end
> The heart-ache, and the thousand natural shocks
> That flesh is heir to [. . .] (*Ham.* 3.1. 56–63).

Note: Citing classic verse plays or poems in the MLA style is an exception to the general method for other works. In parenthetical citation, the section and line for the quotation are given. For instance, (*Iliad.* 5. 22–3) designates the fifth book, lines 22 through 23 of Homer's *Iliad,* or (*Mac.* 4.1. 22–9) designates the fourth act, first scene, and lines 22 through 29 of Shakespeare's *Macbeth.*

Punctuating Quotations of Prose

Quotations of prose longer than three lines of text should be set off by double spacing from the last line of text and indenting the quote one inch from the left margin. The right margin remains "ragged." Quotation marks are not employed, and the quotation is double spaced.

Thomas Mann draws the historical distinction between Wagner and Nietzsche:

> Wagner was the puissant-fortunate self-glorifier and self-consummator,
> while Nietzsche was the revolutionary self-conqueror who "turned
> Judas": and that is why the former was never more than the last glorifier
> and infinitely enchanting consummator of an epoch, whereas the latter
> has become a seer who leads mankind forward into a new age (79).

Deleted Material

Sections of the original quotation left out in the paper should be indicated with an ellipsis and brackets with a space on each side of the ellipsis.

> Thucydides summed up the Spartans' knowledge: "They had intelligence of affairs in the city itself but this intelligence [. . .] came to nothing" (350).

Quotations Within Quotations

A quotation that occurs within a quotation requires single quotation marks.

> As Kochan states, "Ivan the Terrible began his reign and relationship with the boyars as a 'first among equals'" (85).

Language to Avoid

You should avoid *clichés, hyperbole, generalizations,* and *slang.*

- **Clichés** are worn out expressions that have no specific meaning.

  Caesar was **so tired of getting nowhere** with the Germans that he returned to Rome.

  Clichés should be rewritten so that the new expression reflects the specific content of the subject being discussed:

  Caesar **understood that he could not decisively defeat the Germans,** so he returned to Rome.

- **Hyperbole** is language that exaggerates or overstates the case:

  James Joyce's *Ulysses* **is the greatest** novel of the twentieth century, and **everyone** knew that **the minute it came out.**

You can avoid hyperbole by using equivocal expressions that allow for exceptions:

James Joyce's *Ulysses* is **one of the greatest** novels of the twentieth century, and **many** recognized this **after the novel gained a wider audience.**

- **Generalizations** are characterizations that claim to hold for every case when in fact they do not:

All Germans in the 1930s were anti-Semitic.

During the Middle Ages, **every** knight would enter mortal combat upon the slightest provocation.

Often, this can be corrected by avoiding words like "all" and "every" or by using qualifiers:

Many Germans in the 1930s were anti-Semitic.

During the Middle Ages, **many** knights would enter mortal combat upon the slightest provocation.

- **Slang words** (colloquialisms) are terms that are used and understood within certain groups or regions. However, they are not appropriate for use in college writing in which words should be used in their denotative (dictionary) meanings:

Picasso uses an **awesome** choice of colors and a **really cool arrangement of shapes.**

In *The Sound and the Fury*, **the way** Faulkner told the story was **messed up.**

To avoid the use of slang, one should learn and employ the *terminology* appropriate for the discipline:

Picasso uses an **open palette** and an **original composition.**

In *The Sound and the Fury*, Faulkner's **narrative technique** is distinctively **modernist.**

- One of the most common slang expressions is "**a lot of**." "**A lot**" means "an object for determining by chance," "one's fortune in life," or "a piece of land with fixed boundaries." It should not be used to mean "an indeterminate large amount of something." The main problem with using the expression is that, as with most slang expressions, it makes the meaning vague and sounds informal.

Van Gogh uses **a lot of** blue in *The Starry Night*.

Michelangelo produced **a lot of** sculptures for the Medici.

Many of the Post-Impressionists did not receive **a lot of** money for their works.

"A lot of" should be replaced with a specific phrase or "many" (for countables) or "much" (for uncountables):

Van Gogh uses a **wide range of blue hues** in *Starry Night.*

Michelangelo produced **many** sculptures for the Medici.

Many of the Post-Impressionists did not receive **much** money for their works.

Terms and Terminology

Terminology is a group of words specific to a discipline (art history or philosophy, for instance). A **term** will have a specific, "technical" meaning when used within that discipline, a meaning that is slightly but importantly different than the dictionary meaning.

The painting by Kirchner has a very innovative **composition.**

In the study of the visual arts, **composition** means "the arrangement of visual elements."

In the dictionary, **composition** is defined as "a putting together of parts or elements to form a whole."

Diogenes was highly respected by Alexander the Great for his **cynicism.**

In philosophy, **cynicism** is "a movement that advocates a rejection of worldly pleasure and established social conventions as the way to happiness or freedom of the soul."

In the dictionary, **cynicism** is defined as "an attitude that is bitterly mocking and scornful of the motives or virtues of others."

Note on Etymology: The meanings of words have a history and development, the study of which is *etymology.* You should pay attention to the variation of the forms of words, their different spellings as nouns, verbs, and adjectives for instance, and look up words in the dictionary and study the various nuances of meaning. If this is done consistently, you will develop the ability to understand new words from their context and, in turn, will use words with better precision in your writing, leading to clearer and more concise sentences. Also, you will expand your vocabulary.

A term usually retains a certain sense close to the dictionary meaning; however, the nuances of difference between common meaning and terminology is important for understanding the discipline. When you learn the terminology of a discipline, you are on the way to mastering the discipline. Therefore, making a list of terminology for each course and studying that list is an excellent idea.

Section 10

Punctuation of Titles, Names, and Other Matters

The following are some guidelines for punctuation of titles, dates, periods, and styles in academic papers.

Note: It is extremely important to make sure that all names, terms, and other unfamiliar words are spelled correctly.

Titles

1. If the title is that of a *complete* book, painting, musical composition, play, sculpture, or any *complete,* published work, it is underlined or placed in italics. (In this context, underlining and italics are the same punctuation.)

Crime and Punishment	Mona Lisa	The Nutcracker
(novel)	(painting)	(ballet)
Crime and Punishment	*Mona Lisa*	*The Nutcracker*

Rigoletto	*Othello*	*David*	*Pegasus*
(opera)	(play)	(sculpture)	(sculpture)
Rigoletto	Othello	David	Pegasus

For musical compositions, the rule is different. The title of a work that contains the musical form is capitalized but not underlined or placed in italics. However, a work with an individualized title is underlined or placed in italics.

Beethoven's Symphony No. 6 in F, op. 68	Tchaikovsky's String Sextet, op. 70
Beethoven's *Pastoral*	Tchaikovsky's *Souvenir de Florence*
or	*or*
Beethoven's Pastoral	Tchaikovsky's Souvenir de Florence

2. If the title is that of a poem, short story, or any other *part* or *section* of a complete published work, it is placed in quotation marks.

"The Raven"	"The Queen of Spades"	"The Rime of the Ancient Mariner"
(poem)	(short story)	(poem)

3. If the title or name is that of a work of architecture, it is capitalized only.

the Parthenon   the Pantheon   Notre Dame Cathedral

Names, Periods, Styles, Dates

4. Historical events, documents, periods, and movements should be capitalized.

the Reformation	the Hundred Years' War	the Age of Reason
the Constitution	the Renaissance	the Enlightenment
the Romantic Movement	Classicism	Mannerism

5. Adjectives for periods and styles, and the noun form referring to an adherent, are capitalized sometimes.

romantic novel	realistic painter	neoclassical sculptor
Romantic novel	Realist painter	Neoclassical sculptor
a romanticist	a realist	a neoclassicist
a Romantic	a Realist	a Neoclassicist

You should check with your instructor for the style of preference.

6. The Bible, the books of the Bible, and other sacred writings are capitalized only, not underlined or italicized. The adjectival form for the Bible (biblical) is not capitalized; however, the adjectival form of other sacred texts are capitalized.

Bible	Koran	Talmud
biblical humor	Koranic studies	Talmudic scholar

7. The word "god" is capitalized when it refers to a personal god, such as the god of Christianity and Judaism, because then it is used as a personal name. However, if "god" refers to a god or gods in general, the word is not capitalized.

Abraham loved God very much.

The concept of a god was completely alien to them.

The men prayed to their gods.

8. Decades are written with an "s" but no apostrophe.

1620s   1970s   1200s

9. Centuries are not capitalized.

the fifth century BC   the sixteenth century

10. As adjectives, centuries are hyphenated.

fifteenth-century art   twelfth-century architecture

11. Numbers should be spelled out if they can be in one or two words. Others should be represented by numerals.

two	2 1/2
sixty-six	133
one thousand	412

Foreign Words, Possessives, Contractions

12. *Foreign words*, not found in an English dictionary, should be underlined or italicized:

| <u>contrapposto</u> | <u>sophia</u> | <u>histoire</u> |
| *contrapposto* | *sophia* | *histoire* |

13. *Possesives* show ownership and are formed by adding an apostrophe (') or an apostrophe and an "s" ('s).

To form the possessive of a singular noun, you add an apostrophe and an "s":

Camus's *The Plague*   Morisot's colors   Marx's position

To form the possessive of a plural noun ending in "s," you add an apostrophe only:

artists' brushwork   directors' batons   philosophers' method

To form the possessive of a plural noun ending other than with an "s," you add an apostrophe and an "s":

children's books   women's studies   men's attitudes

14. Abbreviations and other shorthand such as contractions and "etc." should not be used.

| **Do not use:** | can't | isn't | wouldn't |
| **Use:** | cannot (one word) | is not | would not |

Do not use: Leonardo was a painter, sculptor, **etc.**

Use: Leonardo was a painter, sculptor, **scientist, inventor, and psychologist.**

Errors are distracting and interfere with the reader's ability to follow the argument of the paper. Grammatically and stylistically correct writing, on the other hand, does not call attention to itself, which allows the reader to follow the ideas without distraction. For this reason, spelling, punctuation, style, and formatting are important matters.

Note: Where there are choices on points of style, the important thing is to be consistent throughout your paper.

Section 11

The Research Paper

Structure

The research paper follows the structure of a formal essay. The main idea is located in the thesis, and the argument is defended paragraph by paragraph. Research papers, however, are longer, so the demands on organization are greater. Consequently, a very good outline is needed, but the thesis-and-topic-sentence pattern should be consistently followed.

Support

The support for a research paper comes mostly from *sources* consisting of scholarly books, articles, and other materials. The writer uses these sources to back up the main points of the thesis.

Documentation

The use of sources must be documented. The following sections give formats and examples for documenting sources in the MLA and Chicago styles for print media and the Columbia style for online documentation.

The Process

The thesis for a research paper should be an original opinion about the subject: a comparison of two paintings by Van Gogh, the explanation of the narrative point-of-view in Thomas Mann's *Death in Venice,* or the relationship between Stalin and Hitler before the German invasion of the Soviet Union. In general, you should form a working thesis before the research is conducted, but the thesis will usually become more focused as you learn more about the subject from reading the experts.

A major and common problem for the beginning student is the tendency to be influenced by secondary sources—expert opinion—to the extent that the student loses sight of the original thesis. One way to avoid this is to develop a good outline. You should keep each version of the developing thesis clearly written down and then organize the opinions of each secondary source in relation to the developing thesis. You will find that the better your organization of notes, quotations, and secondary sources is during the research process, the better your organization of the final draft of the paper will be.

Section 12

Primary and Secondary Sources

Sources are the materials—books, articles, poems, novels, paintings, sculptures, plays, architectural structures, films, Internet sites, for example—that are used in a research paper. The source that is the subject of the paper is the *primary source*. A *secondary source* is one that comments on the subject or is used as background or in some other capacity. Sources are the major focus of a research paper because they constitute both the subject of the research paper (*primary sources*) and the support for the thesis (*secondary sources*).

In a research paper about Faulkner's *The Sound and the Fury,* Eisenstein's *Battleship Potempkin,* or Caesar's Gallic Wars, the primary sources would consist of *anything written by* Faulkner himself; or *any work by* Eisenstein including his autobiography, letters, and any other films; or *any works by* Caesar himself. If you are writing about Monet, *any paintings by* Monet or *anything written by* Monet are primary sources. In general, primary sources are strong support for the thesis because they are closest to the factual. For instance, if Faulkner's explanation of the structure of *The Sound and the Fury* backs up your opinion of the structure of the novel, then this is strong support. Again, if you explain in detail the exact series of images from the "Odessa steps" sequence in Eisenstein's *Battleship Potempkin* to explain the director's use of montage, you are using facts from a primary source, which is convincing support. Finally, what Caesar says about his campaigns would be important and decisive. This might not mean that what the author, artist, or historical figure has to say is the final word—and some writers, artists and historical figures have said little or nothing or even deliberately misled critics—so you need the support of experts to make a convincing argument.

Using the Computer in Library Research

Secondary sources are, for the most part, less convincing as support than are primary sources because they rely on the opinion of experts instead of statements by and facts about authors, artists, and the works themselves. However, secondary sources are valuable and necessary because they are written by experts who have spent years studying their subjects. Nevertheless, when using sources, you must be careful that the secondary sources are, in fact, *valid authorities.* That is, secondary sources must be recognized as authoritative by academic experts. In general, secondary sources consist of books and journals from libraries and, importantly nowadays, material found on the Internet including online versions of academic journals. However, you must be careful about material found on the Internet. (See "Internet Sources" later in this section.)

Mostly today, sources are found through checking databases on the computer, usually in the college library itself. *If you are not already familiar with locating sources through databases or want to become more efficient in doing so, you should consult the reference librarian whose duty is to instruct students on using library resources.* The following are examples and suggestions for locating sources in the library.

Library Databases

Today, research usually begins on the computer. There are, generally, two major resources at the student's command: the university or college *online catalogue* and the university or college *databases* that link the institution's computer network to academic and general resources available on the World Wide Web.

The Library Online Catalogue

The library *online catalogue* is a database that contains all the resources available in the university or college library. Usually, the search engine for the library catalogue is the default screen. This will allow a *simple search* by *subject, author,* or *keyword.*

An *advanced search* screen can be accessed from the *simple search* screen that will allow you to limit searches. In this way, you can find all relevant materials in the library: books, periodicals, media materials, and all other resources.

Online Databases

Databases are usually accessed through a system such as *FirstSearch* and organized according to general area indices such as Arts and Humanities, Business and Economics, Education, and others. Each index subdivides into more specific indices. For instance, the Arts and Humanities general area contains the *MLA Bibliography* for literature, and *Art Abstracts, Arts & Humanities Search,* and *Humanities Index* for the humanities. These databases can then be searched for books and articles in periodicals that are relevant for your specific topic.

The specific system used by the library may not be *FirstSearch* but rather *SilverPlatter, InfoTrac,* or another. You should consult the research librarian for this information and information for accessing the system.

Full-Text Retrieval

Some databases include a full-text retrieval. This means that you can, for a fee or free of charge, print out the article. If this is the case, an icon will be clearly visible on the screen.

Bibliographical Information and Locating Material

When you locate a piece of material relevant to the research project, the bibliographical information should either be printed out or meticulously written down. Then, you can locate the material through the general stacks, the periodical room, or the media center of the library. Usually, the database on the computer will tell you if the material is available in your library. If it is not, you can gain access to the material through interlibrary loan. Many libraries allow you to apply for interlibrary loans through computer access. *Again, you should consult the research librarian about interlibrary loans.*

Evaluating Sources

Secondary sources must be evaluated. In other words, not all information is valid for academic research papers. The following are some suggestions on checking the validity of sources.

Books and Journals

Books and academic journal articles found in college libraries through *FirstSearch* or other academic databases and published on writers, artists, works, history, and historical figures have usually been reviewed by other experts in the field and are, therefore, authoritative. These sources contain documentation and bibliographies that demonstrate an expert knowledge of the subject. These bibliographies should give you further access to other secondary sources on the subject of the paper.

Secondary sources more recent than ten years old are usually considered to represent a more current attitude toward the subject among experts. However, many of the most authoritative opinions about artists, authors, and works are much older than ten years. The nuances of using secondary sources according to their authoritative validity come through becoming an expert oneself. The beginning student should worry less about this and more about finding and using sources that are relevant to supporting the thesis.

Internet Sources

You may find a vast amount of information on writers, artists, historical events and figures, or any other subject for a research paper on the Internet by indiscriminately searching. The following are some suggestions and cautions concerning sources on the Internet:

- Through general search engines such as *AltaVista, Lycos, Yahoo!,* and others, you might find seemingly relevant information on the topic. However, anyone can post information on the Internet, so the information might or might not be authoritative and proper for a college research paper.

- You need to check the sponsor of the Internet site. Generally, if the site is sponsored by a college or university department or is listed on a college or university library database (*not merely a general search engine*), the site can be trusted. Also, if a site is sponsored by a museum or a government agency, it can probably be trusted.

- Indiscriminate "surfing" for information on the Internet and using that information in a college research paper without being sure of the source *should be strictly avoided.* If you are unsure about the source of information on the Internet, you should consult your instructor, ask a reference librarian, or verify the information by consulting authoritative books or articles in the library.

A Final Comment on Research

Nothing ensures a better research paper than your interest in the subject. A topic should be chosen, for the most part, because you are interested in that topic. Therefore, the best research is probably done the old-fashioned way. That is, after you have located the stacks containing the relevant information, you should merely browse the stacks themselves, glancing through chapters, checking book titles, and browsing through bibliographies located at the back of the books.

Section 14

The Use of Sources

In a research paper, sources are documented to give proper credit to their authors and to help those readers who are interested in locating the works cited for their own use. Footnotes, endnotes, parenthetical documentation, works cited pages, and bibliographies are used for this purpose. Generally, three methods are used for sources in a research paper: *direct quotation, paraphrase,* and *major idea.*

Note: If you use material from a source without proper documentation, you are committing *plagiarism.* (See Section 15, "Plagiarism.")

Direct Quotation

When a direct quotation is used, the exact words from the source appear in quotation marks in the research paper.

> In the first lines, Homer invokes the muse: "Sing, goddess, the anger of Peleus' son Achilleus / and its devastation, which put pains thousandfold upon the Achaians [. . .]" (*Iliad* 1. 1–2).

> There are scholars yet today who maintain that Homer was an individual, working alone to create the *Iliad.* For instance, one scholar insists, "The days when romantic scholars believed in folk 'poetry,' producing the *Iliad* by collective action, are over" (Griffin 7).

Paraphrase

Paraphrase is putting the ideas of the source into entirely different phrasing. Usually, the paraphrase is shorter than the original.

> **Original Source:** As always in Russia, intellectual ferment both erupted into and was fed by the novel. The themes of the intellectuals *vis-à-vis* the peasantry are met with, for example, in Leskov's topical novels, such as *Nowhere to Go* and *At Daggers Drawn* and also in Gleb Uspensky's *Power of the Soil.* But it is in the work of the great novelists of the period—Turgenev, Dostoevsky, and Tolstoy—that the full force of Populist themes and types is dominant.

> **Paraphrase of Original:** As Kochan and Abraham point out in *The Making of Modern Russia,* the novel played a central role in the intellectual debates of the late nineteenth century in Russia. Such topical novelists as Leskov and

Uspensky sounded certain themes, and the power of Populism then came to dominate the works of Turgenev, Dostoevsky, and Tolstoy.[11]

The writer must beware of "mosaic" plagiarism. If one merely replaces a few words and keeps the original sentence structure, one is committing plagiarism. The following example is much too close to the original and would, therefore, be mosaic plagiarism.

Mosaic Plagiarism: Very often, the novel in Russia reflected intellectual ferment. In Leskov's topical novels, like *Nowhere to Go* and *At Daggers Drawn* as well as Gleb Uspensky's *Power of the Soul,* the theme of the relationship between the intellectual and the peasantry is introduced. However, in the great works of Turgenev, Dostoevsky, and Tolstoy, the Populist themes and types are the major concern.

To avoid mosaic plagiarism, you should either use the original wording with quotation marks and appropriate documentation of the source, or you should write your paraphrase so that it is entirely in your own phrasing.

Major Idea

When a writer finds a specific idea in a secondary source and uses it in the research paper, that idea must be documented. The major idea often sums up an entire source or a major section of the source. Many times, the major idea can be considered as the thesis for the whole or a section of the work cited.

Kochan and Abraham make the point that writers such as Leskov and Uspensky mentioned Populist themes, but Turgenev, Dostoevsky, and Tolstoy made them central to their works.[11]

You need to be aware of and meticulous about the use of sources because the issue of sources often results in plagiarism. The following section explains plagiarism.

Section 15

Plagiarism

Plagiarism occurs in an academic context when a student submits work that is in whole or in part written by someone else, but the student claims the work to be the student's own. In simple terms, the act is stealing or cheating. Plagiarism is either intentional or unintentional. However, either intended or unintended plagiarism constitutes academic misconduct. College instructors are keenly aware of plagiarism and meticulously look for cases. Nowadays, there are Internet sites that help instructors find student papers that are taken or sold from the Internet for the purpose of plagiarism.

Intentional Plagiarism

Intentional plagiarism occurs when a student turns in a paper written by a fellow student or taken from the Internet, or when a student deliberately copies sections from a secondary source without documenting the source.

Unintentional Plagiarism

Unintentional plagiarism usually occurs when a student uses a secondary source and fails to properly document that source because the student does not understand the proper documentation of sources.

Punishment for Plagiarism

Traditionally, the punishment for plagiarism has been expulsion from college and remains so at some schools. In most cases today, plagiarism is punished by a failing grade for the course, or at least the assignment, with *a note placed on the permanent record of the student's college work*. Because future employers check potential employees' college transcripts, no student wants to have a recorded case of academic misconduct.

Avoiding Plagiarism

The simple way to avoid plagiarism is for the student to submit his or her own work and to properly document sources. (See Section 14, "The Use of Sources.")

College instructors are experts in their field and generally know the secondary material associated with their discipline. They are also aware of the difference between published prose and student writing. Therefore, college instructors do not usually have a difficult time recognizing plagiarism of a secondary source.

Note: If you have any questions or concerns about plagiarism, you should consult the instructor *before submitting an assignment.*

Section 16
In-Text Citation of Sources

The documentation of sources gives the author's name, the title of the work, the publication information, and the page numbers for the specific support material used from a source. The three methods for documenting sources in the text of the paper itself are *parenthetical documentation, footnotes,* and *endnotes.*

Note: You may find examples of parenthetical documentation, footnotes, endnotes, bibliographies, and works cited pages in the MLA and Chicago styles on the Internet at sites sponsored by university English departments and libraries. However, these sites often give contradictory information. To be certain, you should consult Sections 16 through 22 or the current edition of the printed handbook for the appropriate style.

Parenthetical Documentation

Most instructors require parenthetical documentation for undergraduate research papers in the humanities, and the MLA recommends parenthetical documentation. However, you should consult your instructor for the preferred method.

The MLA and Chicago styles follow the same pattern for in-text, parenthetical references. The MLA style employs a "Works Cited" section placed after the text of the paper whereas the Chicago style uses a "Reference List" after the text. (See Section 21, "Sample Bibliography in MLA Style," and Section 22, "Sample Bibliography in Chicago Style.")

In parenthetical documentation, the author(s)'s last name and the page number(s) are placed within parentheses at the end of the last sentence of the citation. *Parenthetical documentation is always placed outside quotation marks but inside the period.*

> . . . at the end of the day" (Mollington 444).

More on Parenthetical Documentation

1. If the author(s) is mentioned in the sentence, the parenthetical reference does not include the author(s)'s name(s).

   Warner points out that Caesar knew of the situation (322).

2. When two works by the same author(s) are used as sources, the first major word of the work is included in the parenthetical documentation.

. . . the myth of the end" (Frye, *Anatomy* 62).

3. With three or fewer authors, all are mentioned in the reference. With more than three, "et al." is used. ("Et al." is from the Latin *et alii, et aliae,* meaning "and other.")

. . . Shakespeare was well aware of the politics" (Brown, Bright, and Newton 162).

. . . this misconception, however, remains today" (Showalter et al. 422).

4. Internet sources will not often include the author(s)'s name or page numbers. For files with no given author or page numbers, include the file name such as (cgos.html). (See Section 20, "Bibliographical Documentation in the Columbia Online Humanities Style.")

Footnotes

Footnotes appear at the bottom of the page on which the source is cited, four spaces below the last line of text. In the text, the citation is marked with a superscript number ([1]). The number corresponds to the footnote on the bottom of the page. *Notes are numbered consecutively throughout the paper.* For the footnote itself, MLA style uses a superscript number, but Chicago style uses a regular font size with a period (1.). (See "Footnotes in MLA Style" and "Footnotes in Chicago Style" later in this section.)

Dostoevsky's views on nationalism changed as he became older[15] while Tolstoy's basic anarchism placed him in a much different position toward the subject.[16]

More on Footnotes

1. Footnotes and endnotes contain the same bibliographical information as do entries in bibliographies, works cited, works consulted and reference lists. The only exception is that *footnotes and endnotes include specific page numbers for the exact information used whereas bibliographical references only use page numbers if the documentation is an article from a journal or anthology.* The following examples are the most common. (For information needed for other cases, see Section 18, "Bibliographical Documentation in MLA Style," and Section 19, "Bibliographical Documentation in Chicago Style.")

2. When one uses footnotes or endnotes, a "Bibliography" is added after the text in which all works used are listed alphabetically. (See Section

21, "Sample Bibliography in MLA Style," and Section 22, "Sample Bibliography in Chicago Style.")

3. Many word-processing programs will automatically format footnotes for the writer. However, the style used might not conform to MLA style or Chicago style. Therefore, you may need to customize the default program or do the footnotes manually. You should always ask the instructor what style of documentation should be used.

4. Online sources often lack the author(s), dates, and other information. (See Section 20, "Bibliographical Documentation in the Columbia Online Humanities Style.")

Footnotes in MLA Style

In MLA style, the first line of the footnote or endnote is indented one-half inch, and second and subsequent lines are double spaced.

1. **A book:**

   [1] William Shakespeare, *Twelfth Night,* ed. Barbara A. Mowat and Paul Werstein, The New Folger Library Ser. (New York: Washington Square, 1993) 7.

2. **A work in an anthology:**

   [2] Jeremy Black, "Warfare, Crisis, and Absolutism," *Early Modern Europe: An Oxford History,* ed. Euan Cameron (New York: Oxford UP, 1999) 210–12.

3. **An article in a journal:**

   [3] Michael Heim, "The Computer as Component: Heiddeger and McLuhan," *Philosophy and Literature* 16.2 (1992): 307.

4. **An online source (Columbia style):**

   [4] Marc Demarest, "Joseph Conrad and Ford Madox Ford," *Conrad and Ford: The Collaborative Texts.* 1997.

   http://www.hevanet.com/demarest/jcfmf/index2.html (18 May 2002).

5. In the MLA style, subsequent footnotes and endnotes to references already given are handled as follows:

   [5] Heim 309.

   When there are two or more works by the same author, you must include the first major word of the work in subsequent footnotes and endnotes.

⁶ Nietzsche, *Thus* 102.

⁷ Nietzsche, *Twilight* 88–89.

Note: "Ibid." and "op. cit." are not used in the MLA style.

Footnotes in Chicago Style

In the Chicago style, numbers are in standard-sized font and followed by a period, the first line is indented two spaces, and subsequent lines are single spaced.

1. **A book:**

   1. Martin Heidegger, *Nihilism,* trans. David Farrell Krell, vol. 4 of *Nietzsche* (New York: Harper and Row, 1982), 48–49.

2. **A work in an anthology:**

   2. Rudolf E. Kuenzli, "Nietzsche's Zerography: *Thus Spoke Zarathustra,*" in *Why Nietzsche Now?,* ed. Daniel T. O'Hara (Bloomington: Indiana University Press, 1985), 101.

3. **An article in a journal:**

   3. Antonio Tassi, "Philosophy and Theater: An Essay on Catharsis and Contemplation," *International Philosophical Quarterly* 35, no. 4 (1995): 51–52.

4. **An online source (Columbia style):**

   4. Annike Christohersen, "The Critic," *Charles Baudelaire: European Art in the mid-to-late Nineteenth Century.* http://www.ets.uidaho.edu/eng258_1/Baudelaire/Critic.htm (12 June 2000).

5. With notes in the Chicago style, when there are two or three authors, all names should be given. If there are more than three, the first author and "et al." may be used. This includes subsequent note references. (However, entries in "Works Cited" and the "Bibliography" always include all the authors' names.)

6. If there are two or more works by the same author, you must include the first major word of the work in subsequent references.

Note: When a second note refers to the reference directly preceding it, "ibid." may be used.

Subsequent Footnotes

In the Chicago style, subsequent footnotes and endnotes to references already given are handled as follows:

5. Anton Chekhov, "The Kiss," trans. Constance Garnett, in *World Masterpieces: Literature of the Western World since the Renaissance,* vol. 2, ed. Maynard Mack et al. (New York: W. W. Norton, 1965), 1055.

6. Allan Megill, "The Reception of Foucault by Historians," in *Journal of the History of Ideas* 68, no. 1 (1987): 119.

7. Ibid., 125.

8. Kuenzli, 103.

9. Martin Heidegger, *What Is Called Thinking*, trans. J. Glen Gray (New York: Harper and Row, 1968), 20.

10. Heidegger, *Nietzsche,* 99.

11. Tassi, 32.

Endnotes

Endnotes conform to the same format as footnotes. However, instead of appearing on the bottom of the page where the citation occurs, endnotes are gathered together on pages following the text under a "Notes" section.

Works Cited

The "Works Cited" or "Reference List" page is *always* used with *parenthetical documentation* and appears after the text of the research paper. It is arranged in alphabetical order according to author in an identical format to the bibliography. (See Section 21, "Sample Bibliography in MLA Style," and Section 22, "Sample Bibliography in Chicago Style.")

Bibliography

The "Bibliography" is *usually* employed with *footnotes or endnotes* for a reference of books cited in the research paper. Sometimes, a bibliography will contain works that are not cited in the paper but are relevant to the subject. Often the list is then titled "Works Consulted" to point out that not all the works are directly cited and to point out that the writer is familiar with other works relevant to the subject that have not been cited in the text itself.

Note: You should study a documented article from a scholarly journal and a scholarly book in your discipline to learn both the proper use and documentation of sources. Often individual scholars and journals will use variations and combinations of forms. *The major consideration is to be consistent in form throughout the research paper.*

Part Three

Constructing a Bibliography

· · · · · · · · · · · · · · · ·

Section 17

Bibliographical Documentation

· · · · · · · · · · · · · · · ·

Bibliographical citations are found on the "Works Cited," "Reference List," "Bibliography," or "Works Consulted" pages following the text of a research paper. A typical bibliographical citation consists of the name of the author, title of the work, place of publication, name of the publisher, and the date of publication. However, references concerning more than one author, media other than print publishing, Internet sources, and other factors alter the form of the citation. Online sources are covered in Section 20, "Bibliographical Documentation in the Columbia Online Humanities Style," and follow the Columbia Online Humanities style. Online sources are integrated into the sample bibliographies included here. The following examples cover the major cases, and by studying them, the student can understand the logic behind bibliographical citation. However, the examples are not exhaustive. For a complete list of examples, see Joseph Gibaldi, *MLA Handbook for Writers of Research Papers,* 5th ed., New York: The Modern Language Association of America, 1999; *Chicago Manual of Style,* Chicago: University of Chicago Press, 1993; and Janice Walker and Todd Taylor, *The Columbia Guide to Online Style,* New York: Columbia UP, 1998.

Note: Although MLA has its own method for documenting online sources and the Chicago style, lacking a system, defers to MLA, the Columbia style may be incorporated into the MLA and the Chicago styles.

Notes on Punctuation of Bibliographical Documentation

1. "A," "An" and "The" at the beginning of a title are ignored when listing in alphabetical order.
2. The titles of university presses are often reduced to the name of the university followed by "UP" in the MLA style (not in the Chicago style)

although standard abbreviations such as "U of Chicago P" are often employed. "Inc." or "Co." should be left out.

Example: "Cambridge University Press" = "Cambridge UP."

Example: "Random House, Inc." = "Random."

3. When two places of publication are given, the first on the title page should be used.

   Example: "New York and London" = "New York."

4. In "Works Cited" and "Bibliography" entries, inclusive page numbers are provided for poems, essays, short stories, and articles that are self-contained parts of the larger work. No pages are given for a full book. In footnotes and endnotes, each reference must include the specific page numbers. (See Section 16, "In-Text Citation of Sources.")

5. When two or more works by the same author(s) appear in the "Bibliography" or "Works Cited," the author(s)'s name(s) is not repeated. Instead, MLA uses three hyphens followed by a period, and Chicago uses three em dashes followed by a period for subsequent listings. Multiple entries by the same author usually follow alphabetical order.

MLA

Remnick, David. *Lenin's Tomb: The Last Days of the Soviet Empire.* New York: Random, 1994.

---. *Resurrection: The Struggle for a New Russia.* New York: Random, 1997.

Chicago

Remnick, David. *Lenin's Tomb: The Last Days of the Soviet Empire.* New York: Random House, 1994.

————. *Resurrection: The Struggle for a New Russia.* New York: Random House, 1997.

Section 18

Bibliographical Documentation in MLA Style

The following examples are bibliographical citations done in the Modern Language Association (MLA) style.

MLA entries are always double spaced, and second and following lines are indented five spaces. The student should pay meticulous attention to punctuation and capitalization in all documentation formats because there are minute differences between the different forms.

1. **A book by a single author:** Author, title, place of publication, publisher, date of publication.

   Steele, Jonathan. *Eternal Russia: Yeltsin, Gorbachev, and the Mirage of*

   Democracy. Cambridge: Harvard UP, 1994.

2. **A book by two or three authors:** Authors, title, place of publication, publisher, date of publication.

   Gordon, Caroline, and Allen Tate. *The House of Fiction: An Anthology of the*

   Short Story. New York: Scribner's, 1950.

3. **A book with more than three authors:** Author, "et al." (in place of other authors' names), title, place of publication, publisher, date of publication.

   Bowersock, G. W., et al. *Late Antiquity: A Guide to the Postclassical World.*

   Cambridge: Harvard UP, 1999.

4. **An essay, short story, or poem in an anthology:** Author; title of essay, short story, or poem; title of anthology; editor; place of publication; publisher; date of publication; page numbers.

   Murray, Oswyn. "Life and Society in Classical Greece." *The Oxford History of*

   the Classical World. Ed. John Boardman, Jasper Griffin, and Murray

   Oswyn. New York: Oxford UP, 1986. 203–244.

   Tolstoy, Leo. "Hadji Murád." *The Collected Shorter Fiction.* Trans. Louise and

   Alymer Maude. Vol. 1. New York: Knopf, 2001. 605–740.

   Stevens, Wallace. "The Emperor of Ice-Cream." *The Norton Introduction to*

   Literature. Ed. Carl E. Bain, Jerome Beaty, and J. Paul Hunter. New York:

   Norton, 1991. 1062.

5. **An article in a reference work:** Author (if author is given), entry title, title of reference work, editor, place of publication, publisher, date. (***Note:*** If the reference work is well known [*The Oxford English Dictionary; Encyclopedia Britannica*], simply give the date and edition.)

Fowlie, Wallace. "French Poetry." *The New Princeton Encyclopedia of Poetry and Poetics*. Ed. Alex Preminger and T. V. F. Brogan. Princeton: Princeton UP, 1993.

"Joyce, James." *The Cambridge Guide to Literature in English*. Ed. Ian Ousby. New York: Cambridge UP, 1989.

"Nature." *The Oxford English Dictionary.* 2nd ed. 1989.

6. **An article in a scholarly journal:** Author, title of article, title of journal, volume, issue number (if applicable), year, page numbers of article.

Kronick, J. G. "Repetition and Mimesis from Nietzsche to Emerson; or, How the World Became a Fable." *Emerson Society Quarterly* 43.1 (1987): 241–65.

7. **A film or video recording:** Title, director, distributor, year of release. (The main performers, writer(s), producer, or any other may be included between the title and distributor.)

Crimes and Misdemeanors. Dir. Woody Allen. New York: Orion Home Video, 1989.

If a certain contribution is being cited, that person's name should come first.

Harold Pinter, scpl. *The French Lieutenant's Woman*. Dir. Karel Reisz. Perf. Meryl Streep and Jeremy Irons. MGM/United Artists, 1981. 8.

8. **A sound recording:** Composer or performer (according to emphasis), title of recording, composer or performer, manufacturer, and the year.

Mahler, Gustav. Symphony no. 3. New York Philharmonic. Cond. Leonard Bernstein. Deutsche Grammophon, 1989.

Bernstein, Leonard, cond. New York Philharmonic. Symphonie no. 3. By Gustav Mahler. Deutsche Grammophon, 1989.

9. **A painting, sculpture, or photograph:** Artist, title of work, the housing institution or private collection, and city.

Bernini, Gianlorenzo. *Ecstacy of St. Teresa*. Santa Maria della Vittoria, Rome.

Brady, Mathew. *President Abraham Lincoln and General George B. Sherman.*

Library of Congress, Washington D. C.

Cézanne, Paul. *Madame Cézanne in Red*. Sào Paulo Museum.

If a photograph of the work is used from a book, the complete publication information for the source is given.

Bernini, Gianlorenzo. *Ecstacy of St. Teresa*. Santa Maria della Vittoria, Rome.

The Western Humanities. By Roy T. Matthews and F. Dewitt Platt. 3rd. ed.

Toronto: Mayfield, 1998. 361.

Section 19

Bibliographical Documentation in Chicago Style

The following examples are bibliographical citations done in the Chicago style that are found on the "Bibliography" or "Reference List" pages following the text.

In Chicago style, second and subsequent lines are indented two spaces. The student should pay meticulous attention to punctuation and capitalization in all documentation formats because there are minute differences between the different forms.

1. **A book by a single author:** Author, title of work, place of publication, publisher, date of publication.

   Steele, Jonathan. *Eternal Russia: Yeltsin, Gorbachev, and the Mirage of*

   Democracy. Cambridge: Harvard UP, 1994.

2. **A book by two or three authors:** Authors, title, place of publication, publisher, date of publication.

   Gordon, Caroline, and Allen Tate. *The House of Fiction: An Anthology of the*

   Short Story. New York: Scribner's Sons, 1950.

3. **A book by more than three authors** (All authors are usually included, but et al. may be used.): Authors, title, place of publication, publisher, date of publication.

   Bowersock, G. W., Peter Brown, Oleg Grabar, and Frederick Litchberg. *Late*

   Antiquity: A Guide to the Postclassical World. Cambridge: Harvard University

   Press, 1999.

4. **An essay, short story, or poem in an anthology:** Author; title of essay, short story, or poem; title of anthology; editor (translator); page number(s); place of publication; publisher; date of publication.

   Murray, Oswyn. "Life and Society in Classical Greece." In *The Oxford History*

   of the Classical World. Edited by John Boardman, Jasper Griffin and Murray

   Oswyn, 204-33. New York: Oxford University Press, 1986.

Tolstoy, Leo. "Hadji Murád." In *The Collected Shorter Fiction*. Vol. 1.

Translated by Louise and Alymer Maude, 605–704. New York: Alfred A.

Knopf, 2001.

Stevens, Wallace. "The Emperor of Ice-Cream." In *The Norton Introduction to*

Literature. Edited by Carl E. Bain, Jerome Beaty, and J. Paul Hunter, 1062.

New York: W. W. Norton, 1991.

5. **An entry from an encyclopedia:** References for well-known encyclo-
pedias are not listed in the bibliography but are cited in parenthetical
documentation and notes in the following manner: title, edition and
entry.

Encyclopedia Americana, 11th ed., s.v. "population."

6. **An article from a scholarly journal:** Author, title of article, title of
journal, volume, number (if applicable), date, pages of article.

Kronick, J. G. "Repetition and Mimesis from Nietzsche to Emerson; or, How the

World Became a Fable." *Emerson Society Quarterly* 43, no.1 (1987): 241–65.

7. **A videorecording:** Director, title, place, company, date, "videocassette."

Crimes and Misdemeanors. Produced and directed by Woody Allen. 104 min.

New York: Orion Home Video, 1989. Videocassette.

8. **A sound recording:** Composer or performer (depending upon emphasis), title of recording, composer or performer, manufacturer, identifica-
tion number.

Shostakovich, Dmitri. *Symphony no. 6 and Symphony no. 10*. Leningrad

Philharmonic Orchestra. Yevgeny Mravinsky. BMG 74321 25198 2.

Mravinsky, Yevgeny, dir. *Symphony no. 6 and Symphony no. 10*, by Dmitri

Shostakovich. Leningrad Philharmonic Orchestra. BMG 74321 25198 2.

9. **A painting, sculpture, or photograph:** The Chicago style has no guidelines for the documentation of paintings, sculpture, or photography. You
should use the MLA style. (See #9 in Section 18, "Bibliographical
Documentation in MLA Style.")

Section 20

Bibliographical Documentation in the Columbia Online Humanities Style

The examples here follow the Columbia Online Humanities Style.

Documentation of Online Sources

MLA has its own system for online documentation, but the Chicago style does not yet have a system. The Columbia Online Humanities style is offered here as a system that may be used in conjunction with the MLA or the Chicago style.

Online scholarly journals, magazines, and newspapers that have print counterparts should be cited for their print editions. Then the online publication information should be added with the version or edition actually used online.

Documentation of online sources is different than documentation of print media because Internet sites and other online sources often lack the author's name, pagination, the date of publication, and other traditional bibliographical information. You should give as much information as possible following this pattern.

> Author's Last Name, First Name. "Title of Document." *Title of Complete Work* [if applicable]. Version or File Number [if applicable]. Document date or date of last revision [if different from access date]. Protocol and address, access path or directories (date of access).

Online sources will sometimes have virtually no bibliographical information. In this case, you can often find the information by following a link back to the "homepage." Sites sponsored by university departments often operate in this manner.

1. **World Wide Web (WWW) site from Netscape, Microsoft Explorer, and other browsers:** Author, title of the work, title of the site, the date of latest revision, Internet address, date of access.

   > McGloughlin, Bill. "Mary Flannery O'Connor." *Flannery O'Connor Childhood Home*. 1997. http://www.ils.unc.edu/flannery/Bionotes.htm/ (27 March 2000).

2. **File Transfer Protocol (FTP) site:** author (if applicable), title of work, date of original publication (if applicable), any previous publication

information (if applicable), title of site, date of publication or creation, internet address, directions necessary to access the publication (if applicable), date of access.

Tolstoy, Leo. "The Works of Guy de Maupassant" (1894). trans. Leo Weiner.

Eusubius. 2000.

ftp://ftp.std.com/obi/Eusubius/ccel.wheaton.edu/t/tolstoy/ maupassant.txt

(18 Nov. 2000).

3. **Synchronous communication from MOOs, MUDs and chat rooms:** Name of speaker(s) (if applicable), type of communication (for example, personal interview) or the session title (if applicable), the site title (if applicable), Internet address, command sequence (if applicable), date.

Fraisat, Neil. Personal interview. *Villa Diodati.* http://www.rc.umd.edu:7000

(8 April 2002).

4. **Gopher site:** author (if applicable), title of paper or file, the title of the complete work (if applicable), date of publication (if applicable), any previous publication information, internet address, date of access.

Nelson, Josephus. "Elizabeth II: Long May She Reign." 1992. Humanities and

Social Sciences Division. Library of Congress.

gopher://marvel.loc.gov/00/research/reading.rooms/main/bibs.guides/qe2.

bib%09%09%2B (30 Aug. 2001).

5. **Telnet site:** Author's name or alias, title of work (if applicable), title of the full work or telnet site (if applicable), date (if applicable), telnet address, any directions necessary to access site, date of visit.

"National Socialism." *Holocaust and Fascism Archives.*

telnet://freenet.victoria.bc.ca select "Government building" (18 May

2002).

6. **Email, listserv, and newsgroup:** author's name or author's email or login name, subject line of the posting, date of the message if different from access date, discussion list (if applicable), address of list or address of newsgroup, date of access.

Barnes, John. "Re: Anglo-Saxon Verbs." *History of the English Language.*

lpz@ebbs.english.vt.edu (5 April 2000).

7. **Electronic publication and online database:** Author, title, title of software publication, version or addition or other identifying information, series name (if applicable), date of publication, name of database (if applicable), name of online service or address, any other publication information, directory path (if applicable), date of access.

Owens, R. "A Sketch of the Political Structure of *The Republic.*" *Electronic*

Antiquity: Communicating the Classics. 3.5 (1996). *Digital Library and*

Archive. http://scholar.lib.vt.edu/ejournals/ElAnt/V3N5/owens.html

(18 Sept. 2001).

8. **Online reference work:** Author (if applicable), title of article, title of work, any print publication information (if applicable), date, information for online edition (if applicable), name of online service or Internet address, date of access.

Terras, Victor. "Mikail Afanasievich Bulgakov." *Encyclopedia of Soviet Writers.*

2000-2001. SovLit.com. http://www.SovLit.com/bios/Bulgakov.html (8

August 2001).

Section 21

Sample Bibliography in MLA Style with Columbia Online Humanities Style for Online Documentation

Works Cited

Blazing Saddles. Dir. Mel Brooks. Warner Bros., 1974.

Bowersock, G. W., et al. *Late Antiquity: A Guide to the Postclassical World.* Cambridge: Harvard UP, 1999.

Fowlie, Wallace. "French Poetry." *The New Princeton Encyclopedia of Poetry and Poetics.* Ed. Alex Preminger and T. V. F. Brogan. Princeton: Princeton UP, 1993.

Gordon, Caroline, and Allen Tate. *The House of Fiction: An Anthology of the Short Story.* New York: Scribner's, 1950.

"Joyce, James." *The Cambridge Guide to Literature in English.* Ed. Ian Ousby. New York: Cambridge UP, 1989.

McGloughlin, Bill. "Mary Flannery O'Connor." *Flannery O'Connor Childhood Home.* 1997. http://www.ils.unc.edu/flannery/Bionotes.htm/ (27 March 2000).

Pages, Neil Christian. "On Popularization: Reading Brandes Reading Nietzsche." *Scandinavian Studies* 72.2 (2000): 163–80.

Steele, Jonathan. *Eternal Russia: Yeltsin, Gorbachev, and the Mirage of Democracy.* Cambridge: Harvard UP, 1994.

Stevens, Wallace. "The Emperor of Ice-Cream." *The Norton Introduction to Literature.* Ed. Carl E. Bain, Jerome Beaty, and J. Paul Hunter. New York: Norton, 1991. 1062.

---. *The Necessary Angel.* New York: Vintage, 1951.

Tolstoy, Leo. "The Works of Guy de Maupassant." 1894. Trans. Leo Weiner. *Eusubius.* 2000.
  ftp://ftp.std.com/obi/Eusubius/ccel.wheaton.edu/t/tolstoy/ maupassant.txt (18 Nov. 2000).

Sample Bibliography in Chicago Style with Columbia Online Humanities Style for Online Documentation

Reference List

Barnes, John. "Re: Anglo-Saxon Verbs." *History of the English Language*. lpz@ebbs.english.vt.edu (5 April 2000).

Bowersock, G. W., Peter Brown, Oleg Grabar, and Frederick Litchberg. *Late Antiquity: A Guide to the Postclassical World*. Cambridge: Harvard University Press, 1999.

Crimes and Misdemeanors. Produced and directed by Woody Allen. 104 min. New York: Orion Home Video, 1989. Videocassette.

Gordon, Caroline, and Allen Tate. *The House of Fiction: An Anthology of the Short Story*. New York: Scribner's Sons, 1950.

Kronick, J. G. "Repetition and Mimesis from Nietzsche to Emerson; or, How the World Became a Fable." *Emerson Society Quarterly* 43, no.1 (1987): 241–65.

Murray, Oswyn. "Life and Society in Classical Greece." In *The Oxford History of the Classical World*. Edited by John Boardman, Jasper Griffin, and Murray Oswyn, 204-33. New York: Oxford University Press, 1986.

Nelson, Josephus. "Elizabeth II: Long May She Reign." 1992. Humanities and Social Sciences Division. Library of Congress. gopher://marvel.loc.gov/00/ research/reading.rooms/main/bibs.guides/qe2.bib%09%09%2B (30 Aug. 2001).

Remnick, David. *Resurrection: The Struggle for a New Russia*. New York: Random House, 1997.

———. *Lenin's Tomb: The Last Days of the Soviet Empire*. New York: Random House, 1994.

Tolstoy, Leo. "The Works of Guy de Maupassant" (1894). Translated by Leo Weiner. *Eusubius*. 2000. ftp://ftp.std.com/obi/eusubius/ccel.wheaton.edu/ t/tolstoy/maupassant.txt (18 Nov. 2000).

Sample Research Paper in MLA Style

Durspek 1

Scott Allen Durspek

Dr. Milam

Western Humanities

April 27, 2001

Constable's *The Hay Wain* as Pastoral Romantic Art

Romanticism was a reaction to the idealism and emotional remoteness that permeated works of art during the period of Neoclassicism. Nature was no longer considered to be rationally comprehensible but rather mystical and unknowable. Two styles emerged within Romanticism that reflected this new appreciation and emphasis on nature: the Sublime and the Pastoral. While proponents of the Sublime viewed nature as enigmatic and malevolent, the adherents of the Pastoral viewed nature as nurturing and benevolent. John Constable was a master of the Pastoral, preferring to paint simple country landscapes. Constable's *The Hay Wain* demonstrates the romantic pastoral themes of the glorification of nature, rural escapism, and the idealization of country folk.

Constable demonstrates the glorification of nature in *The Hay Wain* by infusing a simple rural scene with a sense of divinity through a careful study of landscape and sky. Often the romantic glorification of nature assumes the attributes of cult worship. Constable suggests that this cult of nature involves the embodiment of the divine in the rural landscape, and he attempts to convey this sensibility through *The Hay Wain*. Therefore, Constable's landscape in this work is simple and serene. It is a peaceful

Durspek 2

depiction of farm life in the English countryside rendered in the natural colors of the woodlands and meadows with a stream gently flowing past the hay wain and the modest cottage. The composition was not hastily conceived, but was meticulously studied and sketched before the application of the paint. Constable believed that an element of realism was crucial to understanding and appreciating the inspirational aspect of nature (Darracott 31–33). His method was to sketch on site, giving his paintings a feeling of immediacy, not the remote sense of being created in the studio. Constable also believed that nature could be rendered both "visually accurate as well as emotionally evocative" (Stevens 117). In *The Hay Wain,* he attempts to awaken this vision of divine nature by portraying scenes that one might happen upon while taking a leisurely stroll through the countryside. The action is not heroic or staged, but quiet and benign. This implies that nature is benevolent and to be embraced. In fact, the viewer is no longer an observer of nature but is a participant with nature. In order to arouse the feeling of divinity permeating nature, Constable also demonstrates the importance of marrying the landscape to the sky.

The sky in *The Hay Wain* presented Constable with a unique way to further illustrate the notion of the cult of nature. The sky is an area of the canvas where he devotes particular attention to provide atmospheric realism and symbolism. He is most interested in capturing the sense of movement and unpredictability in the patterns of the clouds, an allusion to the mysterious attributes of unpredictable nature. The English sky is

Durspek 3

depicted with a complex mixture of white clouds and blue sky being
overtaken by clouds filled with rain. The clouds are therefore symbolic of
the recurring themes in Romanticism of mystery and the fleeting nature of
life. As Kurt Badt says of romantic painters in general, and Constable in
particular,

> Without bothering themselves with any clear conception of
> clouds, they made a thoroughgoing use of the circumstance that
> a cloud seems able to assume any form that the painter likes, in
> order to give their landscapes what they called an "ideal"
> atmosphere (22).

"Ideal" for Constable was to suggest the wonder and mystery of nature.
While the clouds perform this function, color is employed to indicate
nature's benevolence.

Constable's use of color gives a sense of the freshness of an
afternoon breeze, so nature is not the fiery one of the Sublime, but the
welcoming Pastoral. The sun is mysteriously veiled behind the clouds, yet
it offers a golden shimmer of light directly in the center of the composition.
By illuminating the yellows and greens below, the resplendent quality of
light gives nature a distinct beneficence. Thus, the realism employed in *The
Hay Wain* serves to suggest that truth is embodied in nature and is revealed
only after careful reflection about, and devotion to, nature itself. The
blending of color plays a major role in the revelation: "Constable's
'alchemy' was not the usual one of fire, heat and the concentration of

Durspek 4

energy, but one of moisture, cooling, and diffuseness" (Bishop 95). Constable's ability to blend color to this effect reflects the romantic desire to seek out and to embrace the spiritual refuge of nature. However, the most significant reason for this glorification of nature was rampant industrialization.

The Hay Wain illustrates the romantic notion of escaping to the country by its depiction of a rural setting as a peaceful and imaginative domain. Constable reinforces the idea of rural escapism by creating a setting that stands diametrically opposed to the damaging effects of the Industrial Revolution. England was the original site of industrialization, and many believed that to be the cause of society's ills. However, The Hay Wain does not depict inner-city overcrowding but suggests an expanse of land that provides a relaxing atmosphere in which to live. There is no sign of abject poverty, for the bucolic haven depicted by Constable offers a bountiful land of sustenance and opportunity. The Hay Wain does not depict smokestacks, air pollution, and filthy water. Instead, Constable replaces the dreadful consequences of industrialization with a scene of beautiful trees, fresh country air, and a glistening stream. As a contemporary scholar notes, "Clearly, Constable's work can still be invoked [. . .] as a picture of a healthy, harmonious and well-regulated England in the era of micro-chip, national doubt, and environmental angst" (Bishop 178). The serene and stoic beauty of this pastoral scene bears little resemblance to city life but does provide the romantic escape from the madness and noise associated with industrialism.

In fact, Constable is so intent on emphasizing the ideal nature of bucolic life that *The Hay Wain* bears little resemblance to reality. Elevating a pastoral scene to the domain of imagination is another manifestation of romantic escapism. As Ian-Fleming-Williams and Leslie Parris point out, Constable's fame increased as the horrors of industrialism increased (130), making him a key figure in romantic escapism. Attempting to find a better existence, Constable and other Romantics created their own realities. In this sense, *The Hay Wain* implies the harsh realities of city life through their absence, yet it does not illustrate the harsh realities of subsistence farming. So strong was the desperation to escape that the world depicted in *The Hay Wain* is largely a rural utopia, and Constable's appeal here became universal (Bishop 45). This romantic view of the country also led to an idealization of the people who inhabited rural areas.

The Hay Wain demonstrates the idealization of country folk by the use of the romantic motifs of everyday life. "Since nature was exalted to be the living embodiment of the divine, the Romantics viewed those who lived close to nature to possess a soul in union and harmony with the natural order of the world" (Jackson). This led to the depiction of humble, country folk as righteous and worthy of esteem. These simple folk were thought to have found true peace and enlightenment by living a life of humility and innocence. Several motifs are incorporated into *The Hay Wain* that illustrate this attitude. There is a small thatch-roofed cottage in the painting that denotes simplicity of existence. There is nothing elaborate, ornate or sophisticated about this dwelling. The stone farmhouse with a roof made of straw symbolizes that nature, though unpredictable, is benevolent and has surrendered the materials necessary to provide shelter and comfort for this family. Another pastoral motif is the gently flowing stream that serpentines through the painting. Yet again, nature is supplying irrigation and navigation to the common folk who choose to dwell on its banks. There are cows grazing in the background, horses pulling the wagon, and a dog roaming the edge of the water.

Through these motifs Constable illustrates that the folk represented here are also in union with the animal kingdom, suggesting the complete benevolence of nature as opposed to the disharmony of city life. They have domesticated the animals and work alongside them for the benefit of all. This depiction of country folk was in direct contrast to the conflict and competition that accompanied the industrialization of urban life. The Romantics believed that industrialization corrupted morals and led people to act in ways that were cruel and selfish. Laborers in factories were taken advantage of by the owners which led to resentment and unrest, and eventually riots and chaos. However, *The Hay Wain* fosters an image of cooperation and unity among the farmers on this land. As one critic asserts, "The sentient entirety of a Constable landscape, including animals and country folk, is a study in community harmony" (Berring 50). There is no

Durspek 7

need for unrest and strife in the country; there are no negative consequences of industrialization here, just peace and harmony.

In *The Hay Wain* Constable depicts an idealized life as he and other Romantics desired it to be. He incorporates many pastoral themes to achieve his goal of the glorification of nature. The stark realities of the Industrial Revolution that Constable and others attempted to escape caused them to create new domains of the imagination where they could retreat, if only for a time. *The Hay Wain* is an excellent example of the attempt of Pastoral Romanticism to circumvent the inevitability of change. In the view of the Pastoral Romantics, industrialization was a threat to the peaceful existence of traditional rural life. Constable's *The Hay Wain* represents the trend in Romanticism toward a more modern art in the sense that only in the life of the imagination can the idyllic exist in a rapidly industrializing world.

Durspek 8

Works Cited

Badt, Kurt. *John Constable's Clouds*. London: Routledge, 1950.

Berring, David. "Constable's People." *The Accomplishment of Constable*.
Ed. Terry Baker. New York: Albion, 1983. 39–55.

Bishop, Peter. *An Archetypal Constable: National Identity and the
Geography of Nostalgia*. London: Athlone, 1995.

Darracott, Joseph. *England's Constable: The Life and Letters of John
Constable*. London: Folio Soc., 1985.

Fleming-Williams, Ian, and Leslie Parris. *The Discovery of Constable*.
New York: Holmes, 1984.

Jackson, Edith. "Key Ideas of the Romantics." *The Art Index*. 2000.
http://www.eky.edu/pub/u/art/index/jackson/ (20 April 2001).

Stevens, Sarah. "The Realism of Constable's Romantic Aesthetic." *Journal
of Art Education* 77 (1996): 115–24.

Part Four

Analyzing Your Paper

....

Section 24

Analysis of Research Paper

....

The sample research paper in Section 23 is a well-done student research paper that, although not perfect, demonstrates a command of the basic skills needed. The following analysis points out examples for the basic elements of structure and support.

Introduction

The paper introduces the subject by defining Romanticism and distinguishing between the Sublime and the Pastoral. Next, Constable is introduced as a proponent of the Pastoral. Finally, the title of the work introduces the thesis.

Thesis

The thesis contains the three basic elements. The limited topic is *The Hay Wain* and the Pastoral; the writer's position is that *The Hay Wain* does demonstrate characteristics of the Pastoral; and the direction is "the glorification of nature," " rural escapism," and "the idealization of country folk"—all three characteristics of the Pastoral.

Support Paragraph

The topic sentence of paragraph #5 introduces the second part of the direction: "rural escapism." This ties the paragraph directly into the thesis by characterizing the "escapism" as "peaceful." The paragraph develops by opposing the "peaceful" scene with the "damaging effects of the Industrial Revolution," thus reinforcing the "escapism." The point is then finally reinforced with the quotation of the "contemporary scholar" to the effect that Constable's "peaceful escapism" from "environmental angst" remains a major appeal of his art. To the purpose, each sentence reinforces the distinction between the conditions of the city and the peace of the country.

Unity

Each sentence in paragraph #5 speaks directly to the topic sentence, so the paragraph demonstrates good unity.

Coherence

In paragraph #5, the "however" that introduces sentence #4 connects the idea of sentence #3 to the idea of sentence #4. Sentence #3 explains that England is the site of industrialization, and sentence #4 explains that *The Hay Wain* depicts "a relaxing atmosphere." The connection explains the ideas of the two sentences in the context of "escapism." Making these connections clarifies the argument of the paper for the reader. Coherence also occurs between paragraphs. The topic sentence of paragraph #5 contains "imaginative," an idea that is not developed until the next paragraph where it becomes the emphasis of the topic sentence connecting both paragraphs in the context of "escapism."

Secondary Source

In paragraph #5, the quote of a secondary source is introduced by the clause, "As a contemporary scholar notes." The point of the quote is to reinforce the idea that Constable's work in general demonstrates this escapism in reaction to a world that is complicated, complex and threatening. By using an expert at this juncture, the writer is suggesting that his interpretation of the painting as "escapist" is also supported by experts.

Transition Sentence

The final sentence of paragraph #4 introduces paragraph #5. A transition sentence should connect the main idea of one paragraph to the next. The first element of the direction of the thesis is "the glorification of nature," and it is connected to the second element of "escapism" by this transition sentence. The transition is made by introducing the notion of industrialization, which is the cause of "escapism." By doing this, the main idea of paragraph #4 is connected to the main idea of paragraph #5.

Conclusion

The conclusion should bring out the significance of the argument of the paper by connecting the main idea to a larger context. This paper suggests that the escapism of the Pastoral Romantic is part of a larger trend of modern art. That is, the escapism of Romanticism reflects the modern idea that art can provide a life of the imagination to counterbalance a world that is corrupted by advancing industry and technology.

················

Section 25

Editing and Rewriting

················

After receiving a graded paper, you truly begin to learn how to write. Only by correcting mistakes and restructuring paragraphs do you come to understand the interplay between mechanics and logical argument. Just as importantly, only by rewriting awkward and wordy sentences can you gain the ability to write sentences with skill. *Editing* is the process of rewording and restructuring sentences for clarity and conciseness as well as correcting errors in punctuation, grammar, word choice, and other areas. *Rewriting* is the process of restructuring the paragraphs of a graded paper to make the argument clearer. The two processes are interdependent, so you should work back and forth between the two procedures while redoing the paper. The following are suggestions for successful editing and rewriting:

1. An outline, containing the thesis, the topic sentences, and the support, should be done before you write the first draft to allow you to think about and to organize the material. (See Section 6, "Preparing the Structure: The Outline.")

2. More than one draft should be written before the paper is originally submitted to the instructor. This will allow you to correct mistakes in paragraph structure, sentence structure, grammar, punctuation, and format before the paper is graded.

3. The final procedure before submitting the paper is *proofreading.* In this procedure, you should not read the paper for content but, instead, should look at each word individually to check for and correct errors in grammar, spelling, and punctuation.

   Note: The more time and care you spend in preparing the original paper, the less time and effort you will need to spend on the editing and rewriting.

4. When you receive the graded paper, you should meticulously study all grade marks and all comments given by the instructor.

5. When editing, you should concentrate on understanding the errors in grammar and punctuation, and, more importantly, you should learn the rules that cover those errors.

   Note: Only by learning the rules can you eliminate mistakes in grammar and punctuation.

6. If the sentences of the graded paper are so awkward that the meaning is obscured, then you should edit the sentences before rewriting the paragraphs. All sentences marked as awkward or unclear should be rewritten for clarity and conciseness.

7. To rewrite the paper, you should do another outline by writing down the thesis and the topic sentences on a separate sheet of paper. Then you should make sure that each topic sentence logically and directly supports the thesis. Each one that does not should be rewritten to make the support clear.

8. After the thesis and the topic sentences are clarified, you should check each paragraph for unity and coherence.

9. Next, you should carefully reread the edited and rewritten paper for the clarity and conciseness of the sentences, the logic of the argument, and the unity and coherence of the paragraphs.

10. Finally, you should proofread the paper before resubmitting it to the instructor.

Note: Writing is a learned skill. By meticulously going over a paper and correcting errors in mechanics and logic, you will learn the skills of writing. As you acquire these skills, the time and effort required for writing, editing, and rewriting will decrease.

Section 26

Sentence Punctuation

There are three basic patterns for compound and complex sentences. By learning the following three punctuation rules, you will be able to write clear and concise sentences.

A sentence is a *complete thought*. A *clear* sentence is understood on the first reading, and a *concise* sentence gives a complete thought using no unnecessary words.

It is necessary to learn the terminology for sentence punctuation. There are not many terms here, but you must learn them so that you can recognize the different clauses and conjunctions and to use them correctly.

A *clause* has a subject and a conjugated verb:

Tom ran (independent clause)

because Tom ran (dependent clause)

Dependent and Independent Clauses

- An independent clause can stand as a sentence; it is a complete thought.

  Plato and Aristotle deserve human rights.

- A dependent clause cannot stand as a sentence because the thought is not complete.

  because they are men

  "because" is a *subordinating conjunction,* making the clause dependent.

- A dependent clause needs to be connected to an independent clause to complete the thought, and the subordinating conjunction makes the connection.

  Plato and Aristotle deserve human rights **because** they are men.

Rule #1: If the dependent clause comes first in the sentence, a comma is required before the main clause.

Note: For the purposes of the grammar here, "main" clause and "independent" clause have virtually the same meaning.

Because they are men, Plato and Aristotle deserve human rights.

If the dependent clause comes after the main clause, no comma is used.

Plato and Aristotle deserve human rights **because they are men.**

Conjunctions

There are many subordinating conjunctions. The following is a partial list:

after	because	in order that	than	when
although	before	now that	that	whenever
as	even if	once	though	where
as if	even though	rather than	till	whereas
as long as	if	since	unless	wherever
as though	if only	so that	until	while

Rule #2: When punctuating two independent clauses, there are three methods.

1. A semicolon may be used:

    Plato and Aristotle deserve human rights**;** they are men.

2. A period may be used:

    Plato and Aristotle deserve human rights**.** They are men.

3. A coordinating conjunction may be used:

    They are men**, so** Plato and Aristotle deserve human rights.

A *coordinating conjunction* is preceded by a comma. There are only seven of these, so if you memorize them, this sentence structure is easy to recognize and construct.

"boyfans"	**b**ut	**f**or
	or	**a**nd
	yet	**n**or
		so

A clause is a thought, and conjunctions combine clauses; that is, they combine thoughts. Therefore, conjunctions are extremely important because they establish the clear, logical connection between thoughts for the reader, making the writing easily comprehensible.

Caesar defeated Pompey. His soldiers fought gallantly.

Caesar defeated Pompey **because** his soldiers fought gallantly.

Napoleon would have won the Battle of Waterloo. The Prussians arrived just in time to reinforce the British.

Napoleon would have won the Battle of Waterloo, **but** the Prussians arrived just in time to reinforce the British.

Rule #3: Conjunctive adverbs require a semicolon.

Conjunctive adverbs are also able to combine clauses, but because they are adverbs, they require a semicolon. These are punctuated in several manners.

They are men**; therefore,** Plato and Aristotle deserve human rights.

They are men**;** Plato and Aristotle, **therefore,** deserve human rights.

They are men**. Therefore,** Plato and Aristotle deserve human rights.

There are many conjunctive adverbs. The following is a partial list:

accordingly	furthermore	moreover	similarly
also	hence	namely	still
anyway	however	nevertheless	then
besides	incidentally	next	thereafter
certainly	indeed	nonetheless	therefore
consequently	instead	now	thus
finally	likewise	otherwise	undoubtedly
further	meanwhile		

One may distinguish a *conjunctive adverb* from a *subordinating conjunction* because the conjunctive adverb may be moved in the sentence without affecting the meaning:

Plato and Aristotle are men**; therefore,** they deserve human rights.

Plato and Aristotle are men. They, **therefore,** deserve human rights.

A subordinating conjunction may not be moved:

Plato and Aristotle deserve human rights **because** they are men.

Plato and Aristotle deserve human rights. They, **because,** are men.

This allows you to distinguish between *conjunctive adverbs* and *subordinating conjunctions,* so you can punctuate sentences correctly.

Combining independent and dependent clauses into compound and complex sentences with conjunctions and conjunctive adverbs is the basic pattern of written English. ***Therefore,*** *if you take the time to learn the terminology and the rules in this section, you will not only be able to properly punctuate sentences but will also begin to write sentences using these basic patterns. As a result, you will begin to write clearer and more concise sentences.*

Section 27

Sample Grading Sheet

Writing instructors often use grading sheets that break down the major elements of a paper so that students have a good idea of the areas in which they need improvement. This sample should help you evaluate your own paper.

Dr. Milam   Name: _____

Humanities   Date: _____

Paper Grading Criteria

	Poor			*Good*		*Comments*
Introduction:	1	2	3	4	5	
Knowledge of Topic:	1	2	3	4	5	
Thesis:	1	2	3	4	5	
Limited Topic						
Writer's Position						
Direction						
Support:						
Relevant	1	2	3	4	5	
Sufficient	1	2	3	4	5	
Good Paragraph						
Development:	1	2	3	4	5	
Topic Sentences						
Unity						
Coherence						
Sentences:	1	2	3	4	5	
Clear						
Concise						
Mechanics:						
Grammar	1	2	3	4	5	
Spelling	1	2	3	4	5	
Handed in on time:	1	2	3	4	5	

Total Points_____ **Times 2** _____ **Grade**

General Comments:

Section 28

Grading Abbreviations, Words, and Symbols

The following correction marks for grammatical and punctuation errors and for improving structure are not meant to be exhaustive. However, you should study them and learn the rules behind them. Only by making mistakes and correcting them can your writing improve.

The first section is in alphabetical order according to the appropriate word mark. The second section consists of simple marks.

Word Marks

agree.	There is a problem with agreement between subject and verb or between other elements in the sentence.
avoid	Whatever is marked should be avoided.
avoid ?	The use of questions should be avoided.
awk.	The sentence is awkward either grammatically or semantically (in meaning).
coherence	There is a lack of thought or grammatical connection between sentences; there is poor coherence in the paragraph.
con.	The sentence needs a proper conjunction.
c.s.	The sentence is a comma splice; a conjunction or correct punctuation is needed.
direction	Thesis needs better direction.
doc.	Documentation (footnote or other) is missing.
expl.	The point or sentence needs more explanation.
f.p.	Sentence has faulty parallelism.
frag.	This is a sentence fragment; it should be combined with another sentence or made into an independent sentence.
inc.	The sentence is incoherent.
new ?	There should not be a new paragraph.
n.p.	The word should not be in the possessive form.
point	The point being made is not clear.
poss.	The word should be in the possessive form.
punc.	There is a punctuation problem.

quote.	The quotation is improperly punctuated.
ref.	There is a confusing or missing reference; there is a problem between pronoun and antecedent.
run-on	This is a "run-on" or "spliced" sentence. The sentence is two independent clauses without proper punctuation; correct punctuation is needed.
sent. conn.	There is poor thought or grammatical connection between sentences.
sent. struc. s.s.	The sentence has poor sentence structure and needs to be revised.
s.o.	The word should be spelled out; avoid abbreviations.
sl.	This is a "slang" (colloquial) expression or word; use standard American English (words in their dictionary meaning).
sp.	The word is misspelled.
tense	The verb is in the wrong tense.
thesis?	The thesis is unclear.
t.s.	Topic sentence does not relate to thesis.
unclear	The point or sentence is unclear and needs more explanation.
unity	The paragraph lacks good unity between all sentences in relation to the topic sentence.
word	This is poor word choice; replace the word with a better one for the context.
wordy	This is a wordy sentence; there are too many useless words; edit in order to make a more concise sentence.

Marks

ℓ	The word, letter(s), or punctuation should be eliminated.
furniture. Two	The sentences (independent clauses) should be combined with conjunction, semicolon, or other punctuation.
ivory white	The word(s) should be moved.
∧	Something is missing.
⊙	There should be a period here.
⊙	There should be a comma here.
◯	The writer should figure out what is wrong.

?	This is an unclear or confusing point or sentence.
_F_	The letter should be small case.
<u>a</u> =	The letter should be capitalized.
¶	There should be a new paragraph.
✕	Whatever is here should be eliminated.
<u>prize</u>	The word needs definition or explanation, or it needs to be replaced.
(in order to)	The words within parentheses could be eliminated.
fast⌢food	Word needs a hyphen.
can⌢not	Words should not be spaced; close up word.

Part Five

Appendixes

· · · · · · · · · · · · · · · · ·

Appendix One

How to Study in College

· · · · · · · · · · · · · · · · ·

Each course that a student takes is different; therefore, each course usually requires different study strategies. However, certain matters are always relevant. Some of the following may seem obvious. Here, nevertheless, are a few suggestions.

1. **College work requires more effort than high school work.** College should be difficult and certainly more difficult than high school. Consequently, the student should be prepared to put much more time and effort into studying in college. Giving up or reducing leisure time and activities to spend more time on college work is required if the student wants to excel.

2. **Consult the instructor.** Acquiring skills and knowledge is not a passive activity. Often, college instructors will not explain in detail—or explain at all—how or what you should study. On the other hand, instructors are usually willing to discuss such matters outside of class or during office hours. The serious student will take advantage of such opportunities to consult with the instructor.

3. **Use the syllabus.** Usually, instructors put much time and effort into syllabi, and the syllabus for a course contains most of the information you need concerning examination dates, paper due dates, and dates for reading class material. You should keep all syllabi in a convenient location and consult them before and after each class meeting.

4. **Establish a good place and time to study.** Libraries and other public campus buildings are often much quieter and more comfortable for study than college dormitory rooms. Finding a place that is conducive to quiet study is an excellent idea. In addition, you should try to spend as much time as possible studying while fresh. The human mind

understands, absorbs, and remembers material much more efficiently when it is not tired.

5. **Go to class.** Even if an instructor does not take attendance, you should be at each class meeting. Besides reading all course material and completing all assignments, attending each class meeting is probably the most crucial factor in determining how successful you will be in a course. It cannot be stressed strongly enough how important it is to understand the course material in the context of class meetings.

Appendix Two
How to Read
••••••••••••••••

Regardless of modern technology and some current attitudes, the quality of a college education rests primarily on the ability to read and write; that is, on how much and how well a student reads and is able to present ideas in concise, clear, and correct prose. If a student does not read in depth and with comprehension in college, that student will learn little and will never be "educated" in the true sense of the word. The following suggestions for reading effectively on a college level apply to textbooks, works of fiction, theory, and any other reading.

1. **Read with purpose.** All texts in college are—or should be—read from a certain perspective for a certain purpose. If the instructor does not make this clear, then you should ask for the purpose of the reading before reading the assignment.

2. **Never skip an introduction or preface.** Nearly all texts have a preface, an introduction, or both, and these are important for placing the book in context. They usually contain biographical, historical, and other information that will help you to comprehend the reading.

3. **Never read a text without taking notes or underlining.** When the instructor has established the purpose of the reading, you should mark passages that relate to the purpose. You should also mark passages that are central to the plot, characterization, theme, or style of the work.

4. **Reread important passages before and after class.** After you have read the text, you should go back and reread marked passages. Then before the class meeting to discuss the work, you should reread those passages. Finally, after class discussion, you should go over the text once again. In a novel of several hundred pages, a review of key passages only takes fifteen or twenty minutes. To review in this manner gives you a good command of the work for class discussion, papers, and examinations—even for a more personally rewarding understanding of the work itself.

5. **Always bring the book to class.** This sounds simple, but students often come to class to discuss a work without the book. In fact, it is a good idea to bring the last read work and the next-to-read work in case the instructor refers back to the previous or previews the next.

6. **You should always read with a dictionary readily available and always look up a word that you do not understand.** This point cannot be emphasized enough because a student only comes to know a discipline after the terminology has been mastered. *How well educated one becomes is reflected in the size of one's vocabulary.*

Appendix Three

How to Read a Textbook

The following are some suggestions specifically for reading a textbook so that the student can gain the most in comprehension.

1. **Always preview the chapter.** Before actually reading a chapter, you should look at the title of the chapter and the headings. If there are any words or key terms that you do not understand, you should look them up in the glossary at the back of the textbook or in a standard dictionary. Then, you should find any terms that are in bold in the text and look them up. In this way, you will understand the reading better because you will have a general framework for organizing the new material.

2. **Read first without underlining.** Ideally, you should read the chapter the first time without underlining or taking notes. This will allow you to grasp the chapter in its entirety without having to try to memorize specific material.

3. **Mark key passages on the second reading.** On the second reading, you should underline key passages. The best way to locate key passages is to look for a thesis at the beginning of the chapter and, then, locate topic sentences for each paragraph. Also, on the second reading you should underline all key terms, or keep them on a separate sheet of paper.

4. **Review on a regular basis.** For review, you should look over chapter headings and underlined passages and review key terminology before you read the next chapter in a textbook. Also, you should review all chapters weekly and, of course, before examinations.

Note: Retention of material depends on repetition. That is, successful retention of material is a matter of how many times one reviews the material. Therefore, if you go over chapters previously read and discussed on a regular (weekly) basis, you will be very likely to have a good command of the material by the end of the semester. Further, you will retain the material for a long time after the course has ended.

Appendix Four

How to Take Notes

In general, students do not understand the most efficient manner in which to take class notes because they are never taught. Taking notes is usually a personal matter; what works for one student will not necessarily work for the next. Nevertheless, the following elements of taking notes should be observed.

1. **Take fewer notes and listen more attentively.** When one is taking notes, one is not listening well. It is much more effective to listen attentively and take notes when there are lulls in the lecture than to try to write everything down.

2. **Never leave sentence fragments.** You should try to write in complete sentences because a complete sentence is a complete thought. If the notes are merely a series of phrases and half thoughts, they will be difficult to understand and, therefore, of little value.

3. **Review notes before and after each class meeting.** After each lecture, you should review the notes. This is the opportunity to rewrite the notes into full sentences and put them into an outline in order to make them truly valuable study aids.

4. **Review notes at intervals.** You should review notes on a weekly basis as well as after each class. Understanding and remembering information is greatly facilitated through repetition, and it does not take much time to review notes. By reviewing after each class and on a weekly basis, you will learn the material well and retain it better than merely studying for two days before an examination.

5. **Never rely on another student's notes.** One of the great college fallacies is that a student can make up for a missed class by copying another student's notes. Notes are personal, and often students do not take good notes. As a result, relying on another student's notes can often be more detrimental than helpful. *The key is to not miss class.*

Appendix Five

How to Answer an Essay Question

Most essay questions require a single paragraph answer. The structure of your answer should follow the basic thesis-support structure of the writing described in this handbook with the following variations.

1. The thesis of the answer should be a rephrasing of the question with the addition of the direction. The direction is the information that the instructor expects in the response. By rephrasing the question, you will direct yourself to answer the question and not give irrelevant information.

   Question: Name three principle features of the Gothic cathedral and briefly describe them.

   Thesis: Three principle features of the Gothic cathedral are the nave arcade, the flying buttress, and the gargoyle.

   From the thesis, you would describe the three named features in order.

   Question: How does Sophocles build suspense in *Oedipus the King*?

   Thesis: Sophocles builds suspense in *Oedipus the King* by establishing the greatness of Oedipus and delaying his knowledge of the identity of his parents.

   The body of the answer would explain how Sophocles accomplishes these two things.

2. Essay answers should be short and to the point. Therefore, the thesis should be the first sentence and the explanation should directly follow.

Index